When the road ahead
is winding and unfamiliar
and we wonder what fate awaits us,
we remember we don't walk alone.
God will never leave us or forsake us,
and He will be with us wherever we go.

*And there is hope
for a woman's heart.*

Hope for a Woman's Heart

HOPE
for a
WOMAN'S HEART

52 encouraging devotions

PAM TEBOW

TYNDALE
MOMENTUM®

The Tyndale nonfiction imprint

Visit Tyndale online at tyndale.com.

Visit Tyndale Momentum online at tyndalemomentum.com.

TYNDALE, Tyndale's quill logo, *Tyndale Momentum*, and the Tyndale Momentum logo are registered trademarks of Tyndale House Ministries. Tyndale Momentum is the nonfiction imprint of Tyndale House Publishers, Carol Stream, Illinois.

Hope for a Woman's Heart: 52 Encouraging Devotions

Designed by Julie Chen

Edited by Karin Stock Buursma

Published in association with the literary agency of The Fedd Agency, Inc., P.O. Box 341973, Austin, TX 78734.

For information about special discounts for bulk purchases, please contact Tyndale House Publishers at csresponse@tyndale.com, or call 1-855-277-9400.

ISBN 978-1-4964-3136-3

Printed in China

27   26   25   24   23   22   21
7   6   5   4   3   2   1

Although these devotions were written to

encourage women, this book is dedicated to

my husband, Bob, who encourages me—with

his passionate love for our family, for God

and His Word, and for reaching the lost with

the gospel. I have loved you for fifty years!

CONTENTS

INTRODUCTION

WHEN OUR PLANS ARE UNFULFILLED and the future holds no promise, we cling to the promises of God, who has plans for our welfare, plans for our future, and plans to give us hope (Jeremiah 29:11).

And there is hope for a woman's heart.

When our energy is depleted and we're tempted to give up, we place our hope in the Lord, and He gives us new strength to walk, run, and not get weary (Isaiah 40:31).

And there is hope for a woman's heart.

When the road ahead is winding and unfamiliar and we wonder what fate awaits us, we remember we don't walk alone. God will never leave us or forsake us, and He will be with us wherever we go (Matthew 28:20; Joshua 1:9).

And there is hope for a woman's heart.

When the economic outlook rises and falls like waves of the sea, we can be sure that our lasting hope in Jesus is the anchor of our souls, a hope both sure and steadfast (Hebrews 6:19-20).

And there is hope for a woman's heart.

When we're paralyzed by regret, we leave the past behind and reach forward to the future with assurance that if we confess our sins, He forgives every one and removes them as far as the east is from the west (1 John 1:9; Psalm 103:12).

And there is hope for a woman's heart.

When our burdens are so heavy that we stumble under the load, we hear our Savior say, "Come to Me, all who are weary and heavy-laden, and I will give you rest. Take my yoke upon you and learn from Me, for I am gentle and humble in heart, and you will find rest for your souls" (Matthew 11:28-29).

And there is hope for a woman's heart.

When loss and grief overwhelm us, we are comforted by the God of all comfort, and we don't grieve like those who have no hope, for we'll always be with Lord (1 Thessalonians 4:13-18).

And there is hope for a woman's heart.

When we wonder whether God loves us, even though He knows everything about us, He assures us we are saved by His grace, not because of our deeds (Titus 3:5-7). And He doesn't lie when He promises us the hope of eternal life (Titus 1:2).

And there is hope for a woman's heart.

When stress and worry consume us, we exchange every anxiety for God's unmistakable peace, a peace unlike anything our world can offer (Philippians 4:6-7).

And there is hope for a woman's heart.

When we've explored every option and our only alternative is to wait, we wait in silence for God only, because our hope is from Him, and we will not be shaken (Psalm 62:5-8).

And there is hope for a woman's heart.

When we get the news there is no cure and nothing else can be done, we fix our hope completely on the grace we will receive at the revelation of Jesus Christ (1 Peter 1:13).

And there is hope for a woman's heart.

When we are wounded and weary from life's battles, we hold on tight to our hope that everything we encounter in life works together for our good and God's glory and that there will be a happy ending (Revelation 21:6)!

And there is hope for a woman's heart.

When we're told that hope is a theory, a philosophy, or mere conjecture, we remember that hope is a person. Christ Jesus is our hope (1 Timothy 1:1). Real, lasting, life-impacting hope is found in Him alone, and there is no hope apart from God (Ephesians 2:12).

There is hope for a woman's heart.

A NOTE TO MY READERS

As I wrote the following devotions, I identified with every woman who desires hope for her heart. I have needed hope throughout my life—when I first came to faith as a child; when as a college student I learned what it really meant to follow Jesus; when I married Bob and eventually became a mom to five children; when my family left everything we knew and became missionaries in the Philippines; when I underwent life-threatening complications during my pregnancy with my youngest son; when we transitioned back to Florida for a life of ministry here and overseas; and now as I watch my adult children find their purposes and raise their own families. I have desperately needed hope in God through all the challenges and various circumstances I have faced.

For many years, I have been blessed to speak to groups of women, and before choosing my topic, I inquire about the needs in the church and community. The response from event planners almost always reveals that their women are desperate for encouragement. Hope is lacking, and "hope deferred makes the heart sick" (Proverbs 13:12). How many of us travel through our days and our lives with sick hearts? We can go on without people, possessions, and purpose for a little while, but we struggle to go on without hope. Women stand in line following my speaking events to share with me their hurts, fears, and struggles, as well as how the message of hope inspires them to believe that God cares about their pain and sorrow. We bond because our hearts are encouraged by genuine, grace-filled, life-altering hope!

Hope is not speculation, wishful thinking, or reserved for the super Christian. And although we face countless disappointments in our lifetimes, we have the promise that "hope does not disappoint" (Romans 5:5). Hope is in the person of Jesus: "Christ Jesus, who is our hope" (1 Timothy 1:1). When we trust Him as our Savior, we are born again to a living hope (1 Peter 1:3), able to see life from a new perspective.

My definition of hope is "a dynamic confidence that God will come through." And I love how my husband describes hope: "Hope is the battery in our lives that charges us with resolve and keeps us going. It is the light that shines brightest in the darkness of trials." The hope we search for is anchored in the Word of God: "For whatever was written in earlier times was written for our instruction, so that through perseverance and the encouragement of the Scriptures we might have hope" (Romans 15:4). Holding on tight to God and His promises yields hope.

As you read these devotions, my prayer is that you will be reminded of the hope that is ours in Jesus. May that sure hope draw your heart nearer to Him so that when you are tempted to give up hope, you will stand firm: "But as for me, I will hope continually, and I will praise You yet more and more" (Psalm 71:14). Let's make the choice, day after day, to choose hope for our hearts!

> Now may the God of hope fill you with all joy and peace in believing, so that you will abound in hope by the power of the Holy Spirit.
>
> ROMANS 15:13

Pam Tebow

1

OVERWHELMED

Did you wake up overwhelmed? Your list awaits. So do people with expectations. The sun is barely visible, yet already your in-box is full, your phone is ringing, and your paperwork is stacked up. If only you could block out all of the above and much more. But you know you can't. You're too responsible, or at least you try to give that impression. You don't want to burden your friends because you suspect they are overwhelmed too.

So what next? Do I allow circumstances and responsibilities to overwhelm me? Sometimes I do, but not today. Too much is at stake, because my heart to encourage you requires that I first encourage me. The Bible is full of encouraging verses, but I regularly return to "my" verses. And I suggest you find yours—ahead of time—before you give in to "overwhelmed" and trade hope for hopelessness, joy for despair, and peace for anxiety.

Talking to ourselves can be a good thing when we speak truth to our overworked brains and discouraged hearts— transformative, powerful, life-impacting biblical truth from God's heart to ours. These verses from Psalm 62 are some of my favorites:

> My soul, wait in silence for God only,
> For my hope is from Him.
> He only is my rock and my salvation,
> My stronghold; I shall not be shaken.
> On God my salvation and my glory rest;
> The rock of my strength, my refuge is in God.
> Trust in Him at all times, O people;
> Pour out your heart before Him;
> God is a refuge for us.
> PSALM 62:5-8

Today I poured out my heart to my God, my refuge, my hope. Even though we can talk to others when we're overwhelmed, God is our true source of hope. He is a safe place to pour out our hearts. He already knows everything we're facing, but He waits for us to come to Him and tell Him about our heavy load. I came to Him this morning and gave Him my "stuff." Although my list is still long, and there are more emails, calls, texts, and problems now than when I started to write this devotion, I now have hope. Hope I can't explain in words. Hope that enables me to keep going. Hope that prevents whatever I wake up to (and all the "add-ons" throughout the day) from shaking me. Hope that stands like a high, protective wall between me and "overwhelmed."

The psalmist shows us that when we're overwhelmed, the solution is for us to name all the specific challenges that have the potential to shake us and to give each one to the Lord. Pouring out our hearts to Him is not the power of positive thinking; it's supernatural therapy. God is never overwhelmed by our issues. He is our stronghold, our rock, our salvation, and our refuge. Whisper a prayer, write a detailed list, or just cry out for help. You can do this while you shower, sit at your desk, or drive the car pool. Don't wait until you've tried everything else. Before you're shaken, trust the Lord with everything that overwhelms you. It's a difference maker and a life-changing spiritual habit. I haven't quite mastered it yet, but I'm working on it.

So when we're tempted to revert to "overwhelmed," let's remind ourselves that our best option is not to pour out our hearts to anyone who will listen. Instead, we're to wait in silence for God only, the One we can trust at all times. And nothing can keep us apart from His love. Romans 8:35, 37 says, "Who will separate us from the love of Christ? Will tribulation, or distress, or persecution, or famine, or nakedness, or peril, or sword? . . . In all these things we *overwhelmingly* conquer through Him who loved us" (emphasis added).

REFLECTION

On my most recent trip to the Philippines, I witnessed Filipino women carrying heavy loads on their backs or strapped to their heads. They stumbled from the weight and shook as they walked. What an applicable visual for those of us who are overwhelmed by the stuff we lug around through our days and our lives! How can surrendering your heavy load to God bring you hope? Read Psalm 62:5-8 and write down each point the psalmist makes about our responsibility to God and then what God does in return. When you're feeling overwhelmed, pull out this list as a reminder of the unending hope we can find in the Lord.

EN-COURAGE-MENT

My daughter Katie received a special gift this morning that made her day. Her twelve-year-old daughter, Abby, sent her an encouraging email: "I love you soooo much, and I was thinking about how thankful I am for you. You are literally the best mom in THE ENTIRE WORLD and I hope you have a great day!"

Encouragement! The meaning of the word is exactly what it sounds like: to give courage. My husband, Bob, explains that the Greek word for *encouragement* used in the New Testament means to be called alongside to lift up another person. We encourage others when we walk beside them to provide courage, confidence, inspiration, aid, hope, support, and more. Genuine encouragement is a priceless gift to the recipient but inexpensive for the giver. Why, then, aren't we more intentional about offering courage to the people around us?

Recently I found a journal my mother gave me for Christmas twenty years ago. I wept when I read her inscription on the first page: "This journal would be a good place to begin writing the book that is in your heart." Although I love to write, at that point in my life I could not envision becoming an author. Mom, however, regularly inspired me with the possibility. I wish she had lived to see her dream for me come true.

We may not know until we're in heaven the positive impact of our encouragement on those around us. Wives, we are the best equipped to express belief in our husbands. They need courage to lead, provide, and resist pressure to compromise in a high-pressure world. Our kids need courage to stand alone against the crowd, to pursue their dreams, and to use their unique gifts and abilities to positively impact their world. Friends, neighbors, coworkers, cashiers at the grocery store, nursery workers at church, and others we connect with all benefit from encouragement!

In our hard, abrasive world that beats us up and puts us down, criticism is common and encouragement is rare. But you and I can determine, by God's grace, to be the exceptions, to be alert to opportunities to give courage—such as offering a smile or a kind word, or sending a thoughtful text, email, or note. We can express interest in those whom others pass by and show belief in those who doubt their abilities or who are on the verge of giving up on their dreams or giving in to temptation.

Paul instructed Timothy to encourage believers whose faith, like his, was tested by persecution (see 2 Timothy 3:12). My missionary daughter, Christy, has a ministry of encouragement to abused, trafficked, and persecuted women in the hard place she serves with her family. Recently she told us about coming alongside these women and initiating the process of healing from horrific pain. She taught them verses like Lamentations 2:19, "Pour out your heart like water before the presence of the Lord," and encouraged them to spend time alone pouring out their hearts to God. The women later shared how encouraged they were that God loved them enough to hear their cries and care about their hardships. Although most of us may not serve on a mission field where persecution is more obvious, we live in a world that is replete with challenges. We have the privilege to walk beside friends, pastors, relatives, and coworkers to provide the needed support and encouragement to keep on keeping on.

Christian leaders need encouragement to stand alone against opposition. The Lord instructed Moses to encourage Joshua, who would become leader of the Israelites after Moses' death: "Charge Joshua and encourage him and strengthen him, for he shall go across as the head of this people" (Deuteronomy 3:28).

Jonathan, the son of King Saul, who was pursuing the future King David, "went to David at Horesh, and encouraged him in God" (1 Samuel 23:16). Think of specific ways to encourage the leaders in your community.

The apostle Paul understood that the early Christians needed courage for the challenges they faced. He wrote that one day Jesus will return, "like a thief in the night," and told them to "encourage one another and build up one another, just as you also are doing" (1 Thessalonians 5:2, 11). Paul not only commended the believers for being encouragers but also instructed them to continue to encourage one another as they anticipated Jesus' return. His message still applies to Christians living today. While we wait for the return of Jesus, our biblical mandate is to encourage and build up one another.

REFLECTION

This week, ask the Lord to enable you to encourage at least one person each day through spoken or written words. In the process of encouraging others, be encouraged that God is using you to infuse those in your sphere with the courage to live in light of eternity.

3

A CLUTTERED HEART

I ADMIT TO BEING A COMPULSIVE "NEATNIK," sidetracked by clutter and mess. Priorities are suspended while I put a misplaced item in the right spot, push in a drawer, straighten a crooked picture, sweep up crumbs, or wipe a messy counter. Annoying clutter in my home distracts me from my primary plan. But what about the clutter in my heart?

Pride, vanity, selfishness, bitterness, jealousy, a judgmental spirit, failure to forgive, and more all distract me from the good plans God has for me. Yet while I rarely ignore the real clutter in my home, I often step over, work around, close my eyes to, or make light of the heart clutter that prevents spiritual victories and spoils my potential for positive influence with people in my sphere.

Take advantage

of this great trade today:

Exchange sin's clutter for God's

forgiveness, freedom, and peace.

Although my goal each morning is to address the clutter in my heart with the Lord, it's tempting to skip the unpleasantness. If left unattended, however, accumulated clutter takes over both our homes and our hearts, causing us to stumble. Even if we shove it in a drawer or kick it under the bed, we're still aware of the presence of the clutter we don't take time to deal with. And this is where the analogy breaks down. We can ignore the mounting clutter in our homes with minor repercussions, but we experience life-impacting consequences when we disregard the accumulation of sin cluttering our hearts.

The "neatniks" in my family are outnumbered by the "messies," but all of us deal with sin's stronghold in our hearts. Even when we know Jesus, we are still sinners who can have victory over sin one minute and then be defeated by our sin the very next. It's a battle we will fight until we go to heaven, and thankfully God's Word includes a plan for daily victory. After Nathan the prophet pointed out King David's sin with Bathsheba, David cried out to the Lord for forgiveness:

Be gracious to me, O God, according to Your
    lovingkindness;
According to the greatness of Your compassion blot out
    my transgressions.
Wash me thoroughly from my iniquity

And cleanse me from my sin.
For I know my transgressions,
And my sin is ever before me.
Against You, You only, I have sinned
And done what is evil in your sight. . . .

Wash me, and I shall be whiter than snow.
Make me to hear joy and gladness.

PSALM 51:1-4, 7-8

I memorized the following four verses and put them to a
simple tune so I could hide them in my heart and sing them to
myself as a reminder that only the Lord has the power to forgive
sin and create in us the clean hearts we long for:

Create in me a clean heart, O God,
And renew a steadfast spirit within me.
Do not cast me away from Your presence
And do not take Your Holy Spirit from me.
Restore to me the joy of Your salvation
And sustain me with a willing spirit.
Then I will teach transgressors Your ways,
And sinners will be converted to You.

PSALM 51:10-13

Take time today to deal with the clutter in your heart. A clean house makes us happy, but a clean heart makes us holy. We have the incredible option to trade the heavy burden of sin cluttering our hearts for the joy of clean hearts. When we do, we can share the wonder of God's forgiveness with others, giving us the privilege to influence those around us to know our great God.

REFLECTION

Do you have a regular practice of confessing your sin (in other words, agreeing with God that it is wrong) and asking for God's forgiveness? If not, take time to reread the verses from Psalm 51. Also, consider memorizing a key New Testament verse on forgiveness, 1 John 1:9, known as "the Christian's bar of soap." It's just what we need to cleanse cluttered hearts: "If we confess our sins, He is faithful and just to forgive us our sins and to cleanse us from all unrighteousness" (NKJV). And we don't need to *wait* to remove the *weight*! As soon as we're aware of a sin, we can confess it and receive forgiveness. Take advantage of this great trade today: Exchange sin's clutter for God's forgiveness, freedom, and peace.

4

THINKING MORE
ABOUT HEAVEN

I'VE BEEN THINKING MORE ABOUT HEAVEN because my dear friend since college arrived there today. Her family and friends are grieving their loss. She's the second close friend I lost to breast cancer this month.

I use the word *lost*, but actually, they aren't lost. I know where they are, and I will see them both again. Tears are falling on my computer as I type, though, because I'm among the many people who will miss these incredible women, both of whom left legacies of faithful service and lives well lived. I can't imagine the physical pain of cancer and the emotional pain of leaving loved ones, but even though my friends fought to live on earth, they knew for certain that they would live forever in heaven.

Heaven is a reality! The Bible tells us so. The hope of heaven encourages people who have lost loved ones as well as those of us who are moving closer to life's finish line. Having an eternal perspective also changes the way we live now, or at least it should. But there's often a gap between what we claim to believe about heaven and what we really believe, which affects the way we actually live here on earth. It's natural to be tied tightly to the things we see (our earthly goals, ambitions, or possessions) while we overlook the invisible, biblical reality of what is to come. Our Bibles encourage us to set our minds on things above (see Colossians 3:2), press on toward the upward call of God in Christ Jesus (see Philippians 3:13-14), and store up treasure in heaven (see Luke 12:33-34). But how do we keep from looking at temporal things, which are seen, and focus instead on things that are not seen? Second Corinthians 4:18 reminds us why that's important: "For the things we see now will soon be gone, but the things we cannot see will last forever" (NLT).

Both of my friends who recently arrived in heaven focused on what will last. They loved and invested in their families. And when their kids grew older, one friend spent her days driving her van through the back streets of town amid drug pushers, starting a ministry to prostitutes by leading them to Christ, getting them off the streets and drugs, and preparing them for a new life. The ministry grew to include women exiting prison. My other friend led the prayer teams for her children's schools and later for her city. Through the years, she served in multiple roles where she made an impact for Christ. Grateful recipients of both women's spiritual influence will join them one day, because they thought about heaven long before they arrived.

God has a special plan for every one of us. Though we have a variety of talents, spiritual gifts, jobs, and responsibilities and are in various seasons of life, we share one commonality: We need an eternal mindset—the big picture of why the way we live matters and why all people matter, giving us a reason not to settle for an ordinary life and a purpose big enough to keep us on track all the way to the finish line.

My husband lives with an eternal perspective, which has impacted our family more than words can express. Bob's priorities are focused on people and heaven. An eternal focus motivates us to store up treasure in heaven by investing our resources in people, who will live forever somewhere. Think about what you can do now to impact your eternity and the eternities of those in your sphere—the difference you can make with financial support, prayer, volunteering for a worthy cause, signing up for a mission trip, or sharing Christ with a friend. Parents have a ready-made opportunity to impact their families on earth to live for heaven, but all of us can affect those around us in important ways. An eternal investment yields eternal dividends, rewards we receive in heaven from our Savior, Jesus.

As I wept for my two friends who died this month, Bob wisely reminded me, "If we could see them now in heaven, we would not wish for them to return." Philippians 3:20-21 tells us, "We are citizens of heaven, where the Lord Jesus Christ lives. And we are eagerly waiting for him to return as our Savior. He will take our weak mortal bodies and change them into glorious bodies like his own, using the same power with which he will bring everything under his control" (NLT). We were created to live on earth with an eternal perspective, because God has placed eternity in our hearts (see Ecclesiastes 3:11).

REFLECTION

How often do you think about the reality of heaven? Consider how you can "set your mind on the things above" (Colossians 3:2) through prayer and Scripture. Decide on one change you would like to make in your life to reflect your renewed eternal perspective and to make your life count for things that last.

5

GRATITUDE OR GRUMBLING?

It was late when I returned to my hotel room. As I kicked off my heels, I heard a baby crying through the paper-thin wall separating my room from my neighbors'. My plan to turn up the air to block the noise failed, since the room's thermostat didn't work. But at least it was time for both the baby and me to call it a night. What a full day: two flights, a late lunch with hosts, a quick change of outfits, my turn to speak, meeting and greeting, and now sleep at last. Or so I thought. As the baby's cries turned to whimpers, the lounge band several floors below began to play their greatest—and loudest—hits.

From birth, our natural inclination is to cry, whine, pout,

and complain when life doesn't go our way. Since our propensity for grumbling is a natural response to objectionable circumstances, a supernatural solution is required. But how do we resist the temptation to permit negative thoughts to give way to negative words that spread like gossip and lice? In order to endure my sleepless night, I needed grace. The same grace I counted on to impact my audience earlier that night would also rescue me from grumbling about annoying circumstances. God's grace in verse form took up residence in my tired brain: "In everything give thanks; for this is God's will for you in Christ Jesus" (1 Thessalonians 5:18).

Nearly thirty years ago, I put this verse to a tune to teach it to my children. As we focused on each word, I began to understand that complaints are against the Lord, and grumbling is a reaction to His plan. What I intended as a verse for my children, the Lord intended for me to live out. God loves me so much that He prepared me with a weapon sharper than a sword to fight the enemy of grumbling. A few days after committing the verse to memory, I walked out of a store and was hit on the head by a heavy piece of molding that fell from above the doorframe. When I gained consciousness, this verse was spinning in my brain. This reminder to give thanks in all things has become my lifeline to trusting God's plan for me, as well as a blockade to my human tendency for bitterness and grumbling—then and now.

You have legitimate reasons to grumble too. Life is full of disappointments and challenges: hardships you never signed up for, dreams that failed to materialize, people you counted on who disappointed you, and much more. In our offices, churches, gyms, schools, neighborhoods, and homes, grumbling is epidemic, but gratitude is rare. Why can't we join the grumbling gang with thoughts like *My family doesn't appreciate all I do for them*, *Why did she get the raise?* or *I'm always cleaning up his mess?* Because when our response to *everything* is to display an "attitude of gratitude," we demonstrate the difference our loving, sovereign God makes in our lives. Choosing to trust Him, when we haven't a clue how our stories will end, affords us significant opportunities for influence as "lights" in our dark world. As we read in Philippians 2:14-15, "Do all things without grumbling or disputing; so that you will prove yourselves to be blameless and innocent, children of God above reproach in the midst of a crooked and perverse generation, among whom you appear as lights in the world."

My gratitude verse continues to impact me as I deal with the long-term effects of that injury from years ago. Recently I quoted it to my spinal neurologist while discussing my

CT scan. He asked me to repeat the verse slowly so he could remember it.

People often ask my husband how he is doing with Parkinson's disease, and he always replies, "Blessed." Bob's response enables him to focus on his countless blessings from the Lord, and it positively impacts the people he greets. One of those is our eleven-year-old grandson, Joe, who was sick for nearly two months while his family was on COVID-19 lockdown in the country where they serve as missionaries. In the midst of his pain and unable to leave his apartment for any reason, Joe was determined to be just like his grandpa and never grumble.

Shortly after I wrote this devotion, Joe and his family were in the last four seats on a plane to America. By God's grace, he didn't have a fever during their thirty-six-hour journey. Although Joe tested negative for COVID-19, he tested positive for parasites and other serious issues that came from living overseas. We are so thankful, though, that through an incredible series of God stories, Joe is now getting the medical help he needs. And he is still not grumbling!

Counting on God's Word and the Holy Spirit who wrote it enables us to make the hard choice, time after time, to choose gratitude over grumbling.

REFLECTION

Memorize "my" verse to prevent grumbling (1 Thessalonians 5:18) or find your own. File it in your brain so you are ready to apply it at a moment's notice. Halt the negative words before they form in your head and leave your lips. When the urge to grumble is overpowering, take a breath and choose gratitude instead.

Joy results from

walking with Jesus, talking with Him,

and staying connected to Him just as

fruit is connected to the vine.

6

A JOYFUL JOURNEY

A<small>RE YOUR BAGS PACKED</small> for a joyful journey? Joy is an essential quality to take along as we travel through life. I define *joy* as an inner delight of the Spirit that is dependent on a relationship with Jesus, not on circumstances.

A favorite joy verse is, "Rejoice [find joy] in the Lord always; again I will say, rejoice!" (Philippians 4:4). Paul wrote this when he was under arrest and chained to a Roman soldier; yet he responded to his circumstances with joy because of his relationship with Jesus. To Paul, real joy was possible all the time, every moment, with everyone, in every circumstance. Always!

Explaining joy is not easy, but it's even harder to live out like Paul did in the midst of life's challenges. My joy bubble bursts when I am crushed by harsh words, when someone I trust disappoints me, and when my long-anticipated plans unexpectedly fall through.

What about you? Were you overlooked for a promotion? Did someone take credit for the job you did? Does your family not appreciate you? Joy killers take a toll. Yet you and I have a choice to make when our joy is tested. If we choose to let circumstances rule our emotions, we will lose our joy. I have searched to find my lost joy too many times.

Joy is not the same as happiness. With the right circumstances, we can be happy, but happiness rises and falls like the ocean waves. Joy is a choice, a decision we make not just once but throughout each day for as long as we live.

In a yellowed stack of scribbled notes, I found my poem about a time when I struggled to choose joy:

I must choose joy!
I can't wait until
My kids are grown
My house is clean
My to-do list is done.

I need joy in the midst of
A new challenge

A midlife crisis
A busy season
A gloomy day.

I choose joy now to
Change my heart
Influence a friend
Overflow to family
Represent my Savior.

So how do we choose joy? The question is answered in the person of Jesus!

I have loved you even as the Father has loved
me. Remain in my love. When you obey my
commandments, you remain in my love, just as
I obey my Father's commandments and remain in
his love. I have told you these things so that you
will be filled with *my joy*. Yes, *your joy* will overflow!
JOHN 15:9-11, NLT, EMPHASIS ADDED

What a relief that I don't need to reach down deep to hoist
joy to the surface like buried treasure, or labor long hours to
conjure it up. I make a choice—I choose joy when I attach

myself to my Savior, and He gives me His joy. Joy results from walking with Jesus, talking with Him, and staying connected to Him just as fruit is connected to the vine. I connect to Jesus and obey the Scriptures in the same way Jesus obeys and connects to His Father. Joy is not an emotion we can fake; it is a by-product of abiding in Christ and being filled with the Holy Spirit. Joy is from the inside out, and our inner joy is evident in our countenance: "A joyful heart makes a cheerful face" (Proverbs 15:13). It is Jesus' joy in us that overflows to everyone around us.

REFLECTION

Take time to commit this short passage from John 15 to memory to make it yours. Then, as you proceed on your journey, make the conscious choice to stay connected to Jesus, whose supernatural joy will overflow from His heart through yours to impact the people you encounter along the way.

7

PRAYER, OUR LIFELINE

WHAT A DISCOVERY! When I cleaned out the attic, I found an old, battered box, a treasure chest full of our family pictures, papers, and keepsakes that had sat unopened for years. Among the contents were family prayer books, listing specific prayers with answers scribbled in the margins. I wept at the heartfelt prayers for each baby. Four of those five babies now have babies of their own.

Over time, our prayers transitioned from handing God our wish lists to submitting to His plans and purposes, even when we didn't understand them. We prayed that we would have God's grace to live the Christian life, love the people around us, and accomplish the tasks in front of us, which at times were overwhelming—like mission field hardships and life-threatening complications during my pregnancy with our youngest son. In desperation, I cried out to the Lord, and He drew me close, resulting in a sweet relationship I wouldn't trade for easier circumstances.

Prayer was my lifeline! Overseas, far from extended family and friends, my prayer life was transformed from a responsibility to a relationship. Like the psalmist, I called out to God: "Hear my cry, O God; give heed to my prayer. From the end of the earth I call to You when my heart is faint; lead me to the rock that is higher than I. For You have been a refuge for me, a tower of strength against the enemy" (Psalm 61:1-3). The Lord became my rock, my refuge, and my strength as I leaned on Him in prayer.

As a young Christian, I thought prayer involved a list of rules, including a specific posture and spiritual-sounding words. In time, though, I realized prayer is simply spending time with God, talking to Him and listening for the whispers of His Spirit. We come to Him just the way we are: wounded, anxious, exhausted, frustrated, burdened, discouraged, or joyful. Prayer can be a mix of praise, gratitude, confession, submission, celebration, lament, requests, surrender, and more. We have the freedom to pray alone or in a crowd and to whisper, sing, or shout. Driving time is especially suited to praying out loud—with the windows closed, of course.

On the subject of driving, no one in our family will ever forget the day many years ago when two cars pulled into our driveway in Florida. An elderly man drove one car, and his wife drove the other. They explained to a curious audience of seven that the Lord had prompted them to give one of their cars to us. We were speechless! We had been praying as a family for another car, but the Lord was the only one we had told. We were all encouraged that our God hears and answers prayers.

When I wake up each morning, I try to remember to give myself to the Lord as a living sacrifice (see Romans 12:1-2). And even though I rarely bow down on my knees, I need to bow my heart and confess wrong attitudes and actions. I ask for pure motives and pray against the schemes of the enemy.

What about you? Are you making time to connect to the Lord in prayer? He invites us to come to Him with stooped shoulders and heavy hearts, to exchange burdens for peace and sin for forgiveness. Talking to the God who loves us unconditionally provides the lifeline we are so desperate for! And it's okay to ask for a car, a husband, or a new job or to pray for a sick friend, our country and its leaders, and other concerns you have.

Do you have people in your life who will pray with and for you? Members of church small groups and Bible studies are known for caring and praying for each other. My girlfriends and I are too busy or live too far apart to regularly connect in person, but because we need prayer, we share concerns via texts or email. Praying friends are the best, as they stand (or sit or kneel) ready to wage war against the enemy and fight for marriages, children, health, and a myriad of challenges. I would give up most things before I parted with my praying sisters in Christ. If you don't have people to pray with, initiate a group and ask for prayer needs. Even if women are hesitant about becoming involved in yet another activity, very few of us turn down prayers.

The privilege of connecting with our heavenly Father is our lifeline and one of our most important opportunities for influence, creating life-impacting ripple effects on the people and situations we pray for.

REFLECTION

As you spend time in prayer today, remember that you are building a relationship with the Lord. Come to Him with whatever is on your heart, and pray for His transforming work in your life. Keep a notebook handy to list your specific requests as well as those from family and friends, and don't forget to record the answers.

8

SHARING OUR BLESSINGS

OUR FAMILY'S FAVORITE THANKSGIVING took place in the Philippines exactly thirty years ago. It was important to Bob and me to teach our children why President Abraham Lincoln chose to make the last Thursday in November a national day of Thanksgiving, even in the midst of the country's terrible Civil War. He inspired our nation to be thankful for the blessings of God, which was also a goal we had for our family.

In our devotions that Thanksgiving morning, we asked the Lord to provide an opportunity to share our blessings with someone in need. Our five children, ranging in age from two to thirteen, eagerly waited to see how God would answer our prayer. A few hours later, we heard the bell ring at our gate. The Filipino girl who worked for us went to see who it was and then ran up the walkway to tell us that a little orphan boy was asleep outside the gate. We never knew who rang the bell to alert us.

When we first moved to the Philippines, we were advised to ignore the poor and the beggars because there were too many of them to help, and they would surely take advantage of our generosity. Our family, however, had been reading a psalm and a chapter from Proverbs every day for years, and we couldn't ignore the Bible's counsel to help the needy. Listed below are just a few of the verses that impacted us:

- "With the kind You show Yourself kind" (Psalm 18:25).
- "Happy is he who is gracious to the poor" (Proverbs 14:21).
- "One who is gracious to a poor man lends to the LORD, and He will repay him for his good deed" (Proverbs 19:17).
- "He who shuts his ear to the cry of the poor will also cry himself and not be answered" (Proverbs 21:13).
- "He who is generous will be blessed, for he gives some of his food to the poor" (Proverbs 22:9).
- "He who gives to the poor will never want, but he who shuts his eyes will have many curses" (Proverbs 28:27).

As a result of reading the above Scriptures monthly, we concluded that our policy would be to give out bags of rice to the hungry and fill prescriptions for the sick—and it was God's business if people took advantage of us.

Louie, a little beggar boy with one eye, was the specific answer to our prayers that Thanksgiving Day. We woke him up gently and brought him into our home. The girls and I continued to fix Thanksgiving dinner while Bob and the three boys gave Louie a bath. They put antibiotic cream on the sores all over his little body and Band-Aids on the worst ones. They tossed his tattered clothes and dressed him in a Tampa Bay Buccaneers outfit from my mom that had been passed down to each of our sons. My mom, a huge "Bucs" fan, loved seeing the picture of Louie in it. Louie had no idea about such things as American sports teams, but he was excited about his "new" clothes. The boys played with him and let him pick some of their toys to keep. They also told him about Jesus.

We will never forget the look on Louie's face when he saw all the food on our table. Although turkey was not available, chicken worked fine. Louie ate and ate. He shoveled food in his mouth with his fingers, and we guessed this was the first time he'd ever been able to eat all he wanted. As our children loved on Louie, they clearly understood how blessed we were and how much we had to share with others.

Louie returned to our house every day for many days. We fed him and talked more about Jesus, while Bob worked diligently on arrangements for Louie to live in a Christian boys' home. But one day, Louie stopped coming. We learned from other street kids that because Louie looked too well fed and clean to earn enough money from begging, his "handlers" had moved him to another part of the city. We never saw Louie again, but our family didn't forget him. A picture of little beggar-boy Louie with one eye is cemented in our brains to remind us that sharing our blessings is not just for Thanksgiving; it's also the Christian life!

REFLECTION

Are you blessed with enough to share? Look over the verses listed above, and choose one to memorize and meditate on today. Thank the Lord for His abundant blessings, and then ask Him for specific ways to pass on your blessings to those who need them. We don't have to wait for Thanksgiving to share what God has given us!

AMBASSADORS FOR CHRIST

WHEN OUR FAMILY LIVED IN MANILA, we became friends with another American family who had children the same ages as ours. The father worked for the State Department as a liaison to our American ambassador to the Philippines.

Our ambassador friends had signed a contract, committing to a high standard of behavior. Their children were warned not to misbehave in public (although they acted up when their parents weren't looking—just like our kids). They all had to follow strict guidelines for dress, activities, and speech. When asked how their family met the stringent expectations for ambassadors, the parents explained that from infancy, the children were instructed on appropriate behavior, and they regularly practiced how to act properly in various scenarios by role-playing at home. The whole family understood that every action and activity would be scrutinized because they were official representatives of the United States of America.

Second Corinthians 5:20 tells us that we are "ambassadors for Christ," so we used the example of these family friends to help our kids understand our own responsibilities in that role. We explained to our children that our lives are not all about us, because we are ambassadors for King Jesus. Our purpose is to represent Him to a world that needs to know what He is like.

In order to be good ambassadors, we also role-played with our kids, but we had different goals than our friends. Our purpose was not to blend in with the people where we lived but to be lights that pointed them to our King. Our behavior needed to match the message of God's love, so we talked about loving people just like Jesus loved us and gave His life for us (see Ephesians 5:2). Even young children understand love.

We also worked on our speech, not only to learn the local dialect but also to think about how the words we spoke reflected on Jesus (see Colossians 4:6). When we left home, we were careful to dress in a way that was appropriate for the culture, but in addition, we emphasized the importance of smiling and being kind to those we encountered. We were blessed to serve in a country where the people are so friendly that smiling came naturally, and we pointed them out as good examples. As I read and taught my children the Bible, the manual for Christ's ambassadors, I learned and grew along with them. We all have a lifelong opportunity to grow in the grace and knowledge of our King, the Lord Jesus Christ (see 2 Peter 3:18).

Because we lived in the Philippines and yet were American citizens, our children began to comprehend that ambassadors live in foreign lands, where they don't have citizenship. "But," we encouraged them, "our real citizenship is in heaven, our eternal home." Philippians 3:20 tells us, "Our citizenship is in heaven, from which also we eagerly wait for a Savior, the Lord Jesus Christ." Even when we lived in America, we explained, the Bible's description of believers as *pilgrims, strangers,* or *aliens* still applied to us, because we weren't yet in our heavenly home.

When our son Robby was young, he loved to call everyone an "alien." It took him a few more years to get the apostle Peter's point that, as Christians, we are "aliens" who don't make ourselves at home here on earth since we are just passing through. Later in life, Robby became an active ambassador for Christ, impacting countless lives with his energizing faith. When he moved to an area of mostly unchurched people, he planted a church in their midst. He also produced a sports-themed movie that scored at the box office; but more importantly, it creatively communicated the gospel to people who might never attend church.

We have an incredible privilege and responsibility to represent King Jesus as His ambassadors. Do we take it seriously? Does it change the way we live and alter our purpose and priorities? Or do we blend in with our world, seeming no different than the people we live among? These are questions we all must consider.

I don't have a list of regulations about what to wear, where to go, or how to act when I get there. There's no checklist or contract. I'm so grateful representing Jesus is not all about rules; it's about a relationship. When our lives are transformed by Jesus, we are blessed to represent Him as ambassadors to the watching world around us.

REFLECTION

Think about the life of an ambassador to another country. How does that image shape your idea of what it means to be an ambassador of Christ? Ask God to help you make any changes necessary to represent Him more accurately to the world. Then read 2 Corinthians 5:20-21. As an ambassador for King Jesus, Paul begged people to be reconciled with God through faith in His Son. We should also be prepared to share with others how they can have a personal relationship with our Savior, the one we have the privilege to represent.

10

ONE BOOK

SMALL PAPER EYES are probably still stuck on the walls of the home we rented in Manila—and on the back of a door, inside a cabinet, and under a bed. My goal was to cement a "Bible verse visual" in the minds of our five young children as they stuck the handmade eyes in every conceivable spot in our house. First we talked about 2 Chronicles 16:9: "The eyes of the LORD move to and fro throughout the earth that He may strongly support those whose heart is completely His." The children's assignment was to cut out and color pairs of eyes and tape them wherever they thought God's eyes could see. For the remainder of our time in that home, we had fun spotting little paper eyes in unusual places.

The eye illustration instructed our children that God sees us wherever we are, even far from our home in America. And as He sees us, He doesn't just support us half-heartedly; He *strongly* supports us when our hearts are completely His. Even the little ones concluded that we really needed God's support.

As parents, our primary goal with children at home was to prepare them for life. Bob and I knew that Scripture was our best resource for equipping our children for whatever God was calling them to. Second Timothy 3:16-17 says, "All Scripture is inspired by God and profitable for teaching, for reproof, for correction, for training in righteousness; so that the man of God may be adequate, equipped for every good work." There's an obvious link between God's Word and the good works He planned for us.

From Deuteronomy 6:7, we learned that our priority was to diligently teach the Bible to our kids at all times. Moses told the Israelites, "You shall teach [these words] diligently to your sons and shall talk of them when you sit in your house and when you walk by the way and when you lie down and when you rise up." I prayed for grace and creativity to carry out my all-consuming assignment; and I'm forever grateful that in the process of weaving God's Word into the minds of my children, God also wove it into mine.

Reading the Bible daily is the best habit we could develop,

but sticking Scripture in our brains, like our kids stuck those paper eyes on walls, makes it easily accessible and ready to apply. We can't anticipate our daily challenges, but the Holy Spirit of God knows exactly how to prepare us with His "inspired" Word. My theologian husband explained to the kids that *inspired* in the original Greek means "God-breathed." Our kids were rewarded, or bribed, with "Daddy's Dollars" for verses they recited every week, but the worth of Scripture in their minds, equipping them for good works, continues to be invaluable. As the psalmist writes, God's Word is better than "thousands of gold and silver pieces" (Psalm 119:72).

When Dr. W. A. Criswell spoke at my husband's seminary graduation, he told the story of a famous atheist who received Christ as his Savior on his deathbed. Just before he died, the man asked his servant to bring him "the Book" from his library.

"But sir," his servant replied, "you have hundreds of books."

The man responded, "There is just '*one* Book'!"

What priority do you give to the "one Book"? There are days when it sits on my nightstand unopened. Yet even when I'm running late, just a few minutes of reading, or focusing on a verse or two, impacts my day. I'm desperate for encouragement, instruction, and truth. My life, like yours, is complicated and challenging. God's Word is "living and active and sharper than any two-edged sword" (Hebrews 4:12), able to change a mindset, point us in a new direction, reveal a sin, flood a heart with hope, and so much more. Why are we tempted to do everything else first and leave our Bibles closed? Because we have an enemy who hates the "one Book" and the God who inspired it. Ignore his efforts. Turn to Scripture and prepare for the good works God has for you this day.

REFLECTION

What is your attitude toward the Bible? How can you remind yourself that it contains the faith-building words you need to get through your life with the right focus? Commit to reading from Scripture each day. Then, as you read, select a verse or two to tape on the wall of your mind.

LIVING WITH PAIN

MY MOTHER LIKED TO TAKE CREDIT for my athletic kids, because, as she claimed, "Athletic genes run in our family." Her father qualified for the Olympics in track. Mom was nicknamed "Speedy." My father excelled in football and basketball. *So why can't I jump high enough to try out for cheerleading, and why does my leg always hurt?* I wondered as I was growing up.

Years later, doctors offered no solution for the nearly unbearable pain I felt during five pregnancies and, later, my difficulty in walking. Multiple X-rays revealed no issue other than noticeable varicose veins. Doctors probably thought I was a hypochondriac. I tried not to bring up the increasing pain, but my friend and assistant at the time cared enough to make an appointment with a chiropractor in our church and insist I keep it.

The doctor prayed for wisdom and was the first to discern that my hip could be the problem. No one had ever thought to X-ray the hip before. He was able to see the right spot for the first time, and he sternly warned me, "Pam, you need your hip replaced, and you need it done NOW!"

Once I knew the issue, I prayed for the right doctor to replace my hip. The first six people I asked for a recommendation named the same doctor, and I immediately made an appointment with him. Although he agreed about the urgency of my hip replacement, his schedule was too full to perform my surgery. I'm not normally pushy, but the situation seemed to call for a little push.

"But I prayed for the best doctor to replace my hip, and that doctor is you! Can you please fit me in?" I pleaded.

He looked at his appointment book again, talked to his nurse, and then responded, "Surgery is scheduled for early Friday morning before my other surgeries." I was so grateful and told him so. I knew the Lord was involved.

What I didn't know is why my surgery would require this doctor's expertise—and just in time. When I woke up from the long, complicated surgery, my husband was standing beside my bed. With tears in his eyes, Bob relayed that I had been only days away from being crippled for life. "Your pelvic bone was almost severed, and the doctor rebuilt it with the bone he removed from your hip. Evidently you were born with a displaced hip."

Do you ever feel like no one comprehends your pain? Who cares when and why we hurt? Who is concerned when we can't figure out what to do next? Who's looking out for us and listening to our prayers? Who has the perfect plan and grants grace for the challenges? Who has our back, our front, and even our hips? Only our heavenly Father.

The gospels are filled with stories of Jesus' compassion for people in pain. He gave His disciples the power to heal the sick (see Luke 9:1). He healed the man with the withered hand on the Sabbath, even though it angered the Pharisees (see Mark 3:1-5). He healed the Roman centurion's servant (see Luke 7:2-9). Jesus understands pain. He was beaten, scourged, and left to die on a wooden cross. And to think He suffered that pain for you and me! He died in our place for our sins.

The Lord has compassion for us in our pain. Talk to Him honestly about yours. He doesn't always choose to heal us this side of heaven, but I'm so very thankful that He worked through my skilled, compassionate doctor in answer to my prayers. When I was still groggy following surgery, my first words to my husband were, "I have *no more pain*." Bob was overjoyed about my successful surgery, but he is resigned to wait until heaven for his new body that will be free from the escalating pain of Parkinson's. He believes God will give him endurance to live with pain until the day when he will see the Lord and all of his suffering will end.

As long as we live, we will be subjected to pain-inducing issues. But even if there isn't a pill to relieve your pain, there is spiritual encouragement. We have a Savior who endured the worst possible physical, emotional, and spiritual pain on the cross. He guarantees that even if He does not heal us here on earth, we can look forward to a pain-free body for all eternity! Revelation 21:4 highlights this promise: "He will wipe away every tear from their eyes; and there will no longer be any death; there will no longer be any mourning, or crying, or pain; the first things have passed away."

REFLECTION

What pain are you experiencing? Does it feel as if no one understands? Thank God that He knows the pain you are going through and will comfort you. Meditate on the verses mentioned above, and remember that one day you will be free from pain.

A LIVING SAVIOR

RECENTLY OUR FAMILY was privileged to take the trip of a lifetime to Israel. It was my husband's dream, and our kids made it a reality. The land of the Bible was everything we had imagined and was made even more memorable as we saw the biblical account woven into each stop along the way.

The days were packed with special moments I wanted to freeze, like sailing on the Sea of Galilee, praying at the Western Wall, and walking on the streets of Jerusalem. A special highlight for me was standing on the Mount of Olives, where Jesus will return some day. "In that day His feet will stand on the Mount of Olives, . . . and the Mount of Olives will be split in

The best news

in all of history is that

"He has risen"!

its middle. . . . Then the LORD, my God, will come" (Zechariah 14:4-5).

While we toured, I was burdened to pray for the salvation of our sweet granddaughter Riley, who was almost nine. Her mom, our daughter Katie, shared that Riley had been wrestling with surrendering her life to Jesus, but my daughter was wise to wait on God's timing and not pressure Riley into making a decision.

Although I prayed for Riley the morning of our last day in Israel, at our final stop I was focused solely on the tomb cut into a rock at the Garden Tomb. Like the others in our group, I was solemn and teary-eyed as I stepped into the cave where the body of Jesus may have been laid after He gave up His life on the cross. I pondered the great sacrifice God made for me when He sent His innocent Son to die in my place. "For God so loved the world, that He gave His only begotten Son, that whoever believes in Him shall not perish, but have eternal life" (John 3:16).

The instant I stepped out of the tomb, I heard Riley sobbing. She ran to my husband, crying, "Grandpa, I want to ask Jesus into my heart now!" When Riley saw the empty tomb, she comprehended for the first time that Jesus had died for her, but He did not stay dead. He is alive! Bob wisely found

Riley's mother so she could share the greatest of all experiences with her daughter—the moment she would admit her need as a sinner and ask Jesus to be her Savior. My oldest daughter, Christy, grabbed her phone and captured images of her sister, arms wrapped around Riley as they prayed together in front of the empty tomb. My granddaughter's eternity was changed in that moment. She couldn't stop smiling afterward. Her burden was gone, replaced with joy and peace.

Whether or not we explore the tomb where Jesus' body was laid, we can know for certain that He is not dead. Luke 24 tells the story:

> On the first day of the week, at early dawn, they
> came to the tomb bringing the spices which they had
> prepared. And they found the stone rolled away from
> the tomb, but when they entered, they did not find
> the body of the Lord Jesus. While they were perplexed
> about this, behold, two men suddenly stood near them
> in dazzling clothing; and as the women were terrified
> and bowed their faces to the ground, the men said to
> them, "Why do you seek the *living One* among the
> dead? He is not here, but He has risen."
>
> LUKE 24:1-6, EMPHASIS ADDED

The best news in all of history is that "He has risen"! Our Savior is alive, and He lives to make intercession for us. If Christ could conquer death, He has all power: power to save us, forgive our sins, meet every need, answer our prayers, rescue us, transform us into the people we long to be, give us purpose and the privilege to impact those in our sphere, and so much more.

After Paul, guilty of arresting and persecuting Christians, met the resurrected Christ on the road to Damascus, he proclaimed, "As Christ was raised from the dead through the glory of the Father, so we too might walk in newness of life" (Romans 6:4). New life is ours!

REFLECTION

Take time to thank the Lord as you meditate on His sacrifice. Then move forward in newness of life and the resurrection power that is yours because His tomb is empty.

13

BEND OR BREAK?

"Blessed are the flexible, for they shall bend and not be broken." I don't remember where or when I first read or heard this saying, but I quote it regularly to myself. Evidently I also frequently quote it to others—a friend even gifted me with a framed calligraphy version. My maxim sat above my kitchen sink for years until it was too stained from soap suds and food scraps to display.

I know it's not a Bible verse, but this truism has certainly helped me get a grip when my plans suddenly change. As I write this devotion, I'm traveling home from a speaking event that I didn't have on my calendar until the night before I flew across the country. Don't get the impression that I'm naturally flexible.

Nothing could be further from the truth. I make my plans, and I prefer not to change them. I keep a calendar and a to-do list. I methodically schedule my days and my weeks. But this Scripture verse impacts me more than either my plans or my favorite saying: "'I know the plans that I have for you,' declares the Lord, 'plans for welfare and not for calamity to give you a future and a hope'" (Jeremiah 29:11).

I can't adequately convey the power God's Word has had on me. This one verse enabled me to abruptly leave the security of a home, extended family, and friends to obey God's clear call to move our young family to a faraway mission field—and then to suddenly move again to another new place two years later, when my life and the life of the child in my womb were both in jeopardy. These were situations I certainly never signed up for!

The Lord doesn't always let us in on His plans ahead of time, but it's enough that He knows them. He loves us and creates plans for our welfare and not calamity. His plans give me a future and a hope. In other words, God's plans trump mine.

Most of us know this verse, but it's so hard to apply it and be flexible when plans change unexpectedly: Your car won't start. The game is rained out. A job is terminated. You woke up with the flu. The rumor is true. The lab report is positive. Most of us had our lives temporarily change course when our communities shut down due to COVID-19. Our usual activities came to an abrupt stop, our finances may have been impacted, and our plans needed to be altered, leaving us with loose ends and unsure about the future.

We head in one direction but all too often are suddenly forced to stop and head in another. It's challenging, even seemingly impossible, to change course and be flexible. There is, however, a promised blessing when we bend and flex and trade our plans for the Lord's. The Jeremiah passage continues, "'Then you will call upon Me and come and pray to Me, and I will listen to you. You will seek Me and find Me when you search for Me with all your heart. I will be found by you,' declares the LORD" (Jeremiah 29:12-14).

Finding the Lord is far better than checking off our lists and seeing our plans through until the end. His plans, which stretch our faith, are like a magnet drawing us to our Father God. When I can't handle life on my own, I fall on my knees before the Lord in desperation. And as a result, an amazing transformation begins: The God of the Bible becomes *my* God, and my love for Him and dependence on Him increase as I trust His plans.

I could never have envisioned the result of following God's plans. My journey to a new land led to a lifelong family ministry with an eternal impact. And clinging to the Lord for my life and the life of my child, against all odds, led to the miraculous birth of our youngest son, Timmy (known outside our family as Tim)—a dramatic story God continues to use for His glory.

What plan or expectation for your life should you give to the Lord in exchange for His plan? Picture yourself laying your plan at His feet. Seek Him with all your heart, and trust what He has planned for you.

REFLECTION

Memorize the "flexible" saying if that's helpful for you. Better still, memorize Jeremiah 29:11-14. Keep it in your mind's file so that when plans change, you can "bend and not be broken."

CROWNS OF KINDNESS

"Night to Shine" is our family's favorite night of the year. On the Friday before Valentine's Day, people with special needs are celebrated in all fifty states and in thirty-four countries. Generous donors provide formal attire, beauty sessions, shoeshines, and limos. When their names are announced, the honored guests, accompanied by their "buddies," are applauded by rows of greeters as they walk, run, or are wheeled down red carpets. They are then treated to a fun-filled evening of dancing, karaoke, and more. The caregivers are also treated to a special dinner. It's a night of kindness on display!

Kindness was not a quality I saw lived out until later in life, and I decided I wouldn't let that be the case for my children.

Kindness is a fruit of the Spirit, and we find "kind" verses throughout the Bible. Here are just a few:

- "With the kind You [God] show Yourself kind" (Psalm 18:25).
- "Put on a heart of . . . kindness" (Colossians 3:12).
- "Be kind to one another" (Ephesians 4:32).
- "Do not let kindness and truth leave you" (Proverbs 3:3).

In the many roles we play as wives, moms, students, employees, friends, and neighbors, all of us have opportunities to exhibit kindness. My close friend Nancy is one example. She passes out kindness like flyers to the people she encounters in the school where she teaches, the stores where she shops, the church she attends, her varied ministries, and the neighborhood she lives in. Nancy asks insightful questions and expresses genuine interest in people others pass by without a glance.

The need for a "kindness ambassador" is even more obvious at times like Christmas, a season filled with stress and flurry. Nancy takes time to greet overworked employees, asking about their families and holiday plans, and she thanks them for their hard work. When she expressed gratitude to an attendant for "the cleanest restroom" she had ever seen, the woman burst into tears because it was the first time her tireless efforts had been acknowledged. We have the privilege to represent our God to a world that desperately needs to see what His kindness looks like!

I discovered a special kindness verse for our guys that is the antithesis of our modern-movie concept of a rough-and-tough man: "What is desirable in a man is his kindness" (Proverbs 19:22). Our sons were required to memorize this verse, and thankfully, they also saw kindness up close as they watched their dad minister to the poor and needy, start orphanages, build a safe house for exploited girls, and devote his life to reaching the lost with the gospel.

On a mission trip to the Philippines with his dad when he was fifteen, our son Timmy got his vision to start a ministry for people with special needs. Timmy was sharing the gospel at a local school, and a boy with special needs was prevented from attending because his deformities were considered an embarrassment. God's kindness is mentioned more than two hundred times in our Bibles, and He demonstrated it again in that small mountain village when two friends of the boy lived out the Old Testament meaning of lovingkindness. They showed loyal love by bringing Timmy to the small hut where their crippled friend lay on his cot, and when our son shared the gospel, all three put their faith in Jesus.

As Timmy ran to catch his jeep, he called out, "I'll see you in heaven!"

Carried by his friends as they hurried to say goodbye to Timmy, the boy who couldn't walk exclaimed, "And I will run to you!" He got it!

That moment stayed with Timmy, and in 2010 he started the Tim Tebow Foundation, which is committed to fighting for kids who can't fight for themselves and serving people with special needs. One of his foundation's programs is Night to Shine, which this year celebrated its seventh anniversary.

At the conclusion of Night to Shine, each guest is crowned as a king or a queen. God also crowns us with His lovingkindness (see Psalm 103:4) and gives us the privilege to influence our world with life-impacting kindness. Whom will you show kindness to today?

REFLECTION

Can you think of a time in your life when someone's act of kindness—big or small—made a difference in your life? In your interactions with others today, think about how you can be kind. Reach out to someone through a thoughtful email or text, say an encouraging word to a cashier, smile at the people you pass, ask someone how their day is going and listen to their response, hold the door for the person behind you, give a sincere compliment, or thank someone for doing their job well.

15

TOO BUSY

It was the busiest week that I can remember. While I transitioned from one assistant to another, both were scheduling speaking events for me. On paper, the schedule looked doable . . . *unless* there was a glitch. *I can do this,* I thought, as I approved the nearly impossible schedule. I justified my busyness since my husband and children also had full lives, but I was a bubble about to pop. I was too busy!

Are you too busy? Do you fall into the trap of believing that being busy is essential for thriving in today's world? When you're asked how you are doing, do you respond, "Busy!"? Are you too busy to prioritize responsibilities, take time with the Lord, relax with family, catch up with girlfriends, or maintain a healthy lifestyle? Burnout lurks around the corner, ready to pounce on overwhelmed, exhausted, juggling, multitasking, chronically busy women. In our fast-paced society, it's easy to get caught up in the hectic busyness of life and to believe "buried in busyness" is the norm, the measure of a successful woman.

I flew to my first event on Monday and then to another on Tuesday. As I prepared to speak Tuesday evening, a violent thunderstorm rolled in and short-circuited the sound system and dimmed the lights. Not exactly what I had planned!

I also didn't plan for the storm's impact to close the local airport the following day. A gracious lady from the sponsoring church drove me to the next closest airport, three hours away, so I could travel to my third event. Two flights and multiple delays later, I arrived at my West Coast city at 2 a.m. Thursday morning, exhausted and minus my suitcase. The one person left at the airport to assist passengers promised to research the whereabouts of my missing luggage. After a few hours of sleep, I showered and put on the previous day's outfit, which worked for my luncheon event. My hosts grew concerned, however, that I might have to wear it once more that evening for the dressy banquet.

Meanwhile, my entire family was in Hawaii. Don't get the wrong idea—flying our family to Hawaii is not in our budget, but a close family friend flew every guest in for his son's wedding. My flight was scheduled for the next morning and would get me there just in time for the rehearsal dinner, but it looked as if I would fly without my suitcase.

While my family and friends were praying, I was transitioning from being a "Martha" to being a "Mary." Remember their story? Martha was busy preparing a meal for Jesus and His disciples while her sister, Mary, sat at Jesus' feet and listened to His teaching. When Martha asked Jesus to make Mary help her with the work, Jesus kindly reminded her, "My dear Martha, you are worried and upset over all these details!" (Luke 10:41, NLT). Jesus appreciated Martha's efforts, but she was so *busy* with details that she failed to focus, like Mary did, on the "one thing worth being concerned about" (Luke 10:42, NLT). I bristle when Martha is overly criticized, because we need a healthy dose of Martha in us to handle our myriad of responsibilities, but we also need the balance of her sister Mary's heart to worship our Savior.

My heart was filled with hope when I gave the suitcase situation to the Lord. Employees at a nearby store helped me quickly find a dress and shoes for the evening banquet, and my hosts were relieved I'd been able to change clothes. The large event was one of my favorites. My heart was full of gratitude, and I slept peacefully that night.

The next morning, as I boarded my flight, I hugged the

airline employee who had spent hours attempting to locate my suitcase. "It's waiting for you at your next stop!" she exclaimed.

When I arrived at the huge airport, I was handed my elusive suitcase, the answer to many prayers. I thanked the Lord and couldn't stop smiling—until I started crying. In the last city I ever expected to hear my favorite hymn, a tuxedo-clad man at a grand piano was playing,

> *When peace like a river attendeth my way,*
> *When sorrows like sea billows roll,*
> *Whatever my lot, Thou hast taught me to say,*
> *"It is well, it is well with my soul."*[1]

My prayer for all of us is that in spite of busy lives, it will be well with our souls.

REFLECTION

Determine to take at least one step today to transition from being a Martha to being a Mary. Take time to reflect on the Mary-Martha story in Luke 10 or another Scripture, and simply enjoy God's presence. Ask Him to help you remember, even in the midst of the busyness, that spending time with Him is a priority today and every day.

16

THE BEST MESSAGE

I WAS SURPRISED when she called and asked to meet for lunch. We had been casual friends during the years our sons played ball together, drawn together because we were both newcomers to our environment. But our sons had grown up, and we hadn't seen each other in a long time.

As I waited for her to arrive, I had flashbacks of our last lunch together five years earlier in the same restaurant. I can't recall the words I used at the time, but my goal had been to make the gospel clear to this woman I might never see again. After some small talk, she listened intently as I flipped through the pages of my little gospel booklet. She responded to my obvious concern for her, but not to the message. Life was too complex for her to add anything else, she explained. I nodded to show I understood and soon left her with the booklet and a hug.

"It's been five years," she said as we were seated at our table. Even before we ordered our food, she began to catch me up on her life, which had been challenging during recent months.

Then I knew it was time—the "elephant" in that room needed to be addressed. I reached in my purse for another copy of the same little gospel booklet, ready to present the Good News again. But before I could say a word, my friend asked if she could have the booklet to replace the one I had given her before, the one that had sat on her nightstand for nearly five years. She showed me the dingy, crinkled gospel tract as she shared her story.

One day, when life was hard and my friend didn't know what else to do, she picked up the booklet and read it. Then she read it again and again and began to understand how much God loved her—so much that He sent His Son, Jesus, to die for her sins. She realized He wanted to have a personal relationship with her. She believed. My friend didn't use any religious jargon but shared excitedly that she is different now. She knows for certain Jesus lives in her heart.

I asked if she had a Bible. She didn't, so we drove to the nearby Christian bookstore, where we flipped through the options and chose one. While her Bible was being engraved with her name, we talked and laughed and promised to meet once a year for lunch. We have kept our promise.

I waited until I was in my car to cry tears of gratitude and joy. All I did was share a small gospel booklet, but God did what only He can do. How incredible that He uses you and me to impact people's lives now and for eternity with the very best message! In Romans 10:14-15, the apostle Paul clearly states our responsibility: "How then will they call on Him in whom they have not believed? How will they believe in Him whom they have not heard? And how will they hear without a preacher? How will they preach unless they are sent? Just as it is written, 'How beautiful are the feet of those who bring good news of good things!'"

When all nineteen members of our family gathered for vacation recently, Brynn and Liam, seven-year-old cousins and best buddies, asked Uncle Joey lots of questions about heaven. Joey wrote and illustrated the comic book tract *Welcome to Heaven*, which I used to share the gospel in the story above. Liam's and Brynn's parents joined the lively conversation, and that night, both grandchildren clearly understood the best message and eagerly prayed a prayer of salvation. If we know Jesus, it's our privilege and responsibility to share the Good News of the gospel. Few life experiences compare.

REFLECTION

Read Romans 10:8-15 for a brief presentation of the gospel and an explanation of why we need to share the Good News with others. Then think about your family members, friends, neighbors, and coworkers. Does someone come to mind who might not have a relationship with the Lord? If you aren't comfortable sharing the gospel in your own words, offer a tract or an invitation to church or to a special Christian event. Ask the Lord for wisdom, courage, and love. It may take five minutes or five years for a person to recognize their need for a Savior. Continue to pray for your lost friends and family members, and don't give up!

COMFORT FOR THE CHALLENGES

Prior to speaking at an event in a large Midwestern city, I was asked to meet privately with a discouraged young woman. I wasn't sure how I could help, but I agreed to try. The woman fell into my arms when I entered the private room chosen for our meeting. She wiped her tears but was too emotional to talk.

"Let's sit down here, and you can tell me how I can help," I encouraged her, pointing to the couch.

After a few minutes, she composed herself. Taking a breath, she blurted out, "I was told to abort my baby." And she started to cry again.

Immediately, tears formed in my eyes. It took a minute

before I could get any words out. "I understand. That was exactly what the doctor told me," I explained softly.

"Really?" she said as she sat up and stopped crying.

"Yes," I said. "We lived in the Philippines at the time, and there was only one recommended doctor in the area. She told me that our baby was 'a mass of fetal tissue—a tumor,' and that if we didn't abort, my life would be in danger."

"What did you do?" she asked.

"My husband and I left the doctor's office and never returned," I responded.

"What happened?" she asked.

I first cautioned her, "Please understand that I'm not recommending our choice without further tests and another doctor's opinion. But," I continued, "it was the only choice we could make. There was no 'plan B' doctor on our island, and we were not about to abort the baby we had prayed for by name."

We talked about the things only women in our situation would understand. We even laughed at the unhelpful comments we'd both received from well-meaning people and finished each other's sentences as we discussed the hard stuff. Then we prayed together. This woman knew I understood how she felt. She hugged me again before I had to leave to speak to the assembled group, and neither of us wanted to let go.

It's hard to put into words the love God gave me for this

woman I had just met. I felt as if a piece of my heart went with that precious pregnant woman when she left the room.

Earlier in my life, I wouldn't have had much to say to her. What made the difference? I had experienced what she was experiencing. I remember feeling alone and afraid when my life and pregnancy were threatened. Only my husband supported me. In human terms, the odds were not in my favor. They weren't in hers either, but God was able to help me comfort her.

When the woman left the room, she expressed that for the first time since getting this devastating recommendation about her baby, she sensed peace. She was eager to see her husband, who greeted us at the door and wrapped his arms around his wife. He graciously thanked me for my time.

I'm not a trained counselor. My spiritual gift is not mercy. I don't know the correct medical terms. But I was able to comfort that hurting woman because the Father of all comforts had comforted me in a similar situation. Second Corinthians 1:3-4 says, "Blessed be the God and Father of our Lord Jesus Christ, the Father of mercies and God of all comfort, who comforts us in all our affliction so that we will be able to comfort those who are in any affliction with the comfort with which we ourselves are comforted by God."

What hard things have you faced, or are you facing now, that God can use to enable you to comfort someone with similar challenges? God loves us, and He has a plan to use difficulties for our good and the good of others. I don't know the end of this woman's story, and I don't know your story either. But God wrote each of our stories, and He is trustworthy. He can use everything we face for His glory.

REFLECTION

Read 2 Corinthians 1:3-7. In our fast-paced society, we rarely stop long enough to listen to someone's story. Ask the Lord for sensitivity, compassion, and the wisdom to be able to comfort others who are going through something you have experienced.

18

THE GIFT OF GRACE

Our ninth grandchild, Charlotte Grace, was born as I was writing this devotion. Another sweet granddaughter is named Riley Grace. *Grace* is not a word I remember hearing when I was growing up, but it is a special gift I treasure now.

Grace is a foreign concept in a world that measures worth by performance. I grew up in that world. Perhaps you did too—and you may live in it even now. As you think about the merits of grace, imagine what it would be like to move into a world where you can fall, fail, or flounder, and grace enables you to get up and keep going.

There are many definitions of grace, but my favorite is

"unmerited favor." We are blessed with a gift we can't afford and do not deserve. Salvation is the supreme example of grace: "By grace you have been saved through faith; and that not of yourselves, *it is the gift of God*; not as a result of works, so that no one may boast" (Ephesians 2:8-9, emphasis added). Our salvation is a free gift, wrapped in God's love and purchased for a high price—the life of His Son. God gets all the credit, so we have no bragging rights.

Grace doesn't stop at salvation, though. God promises grace for every day—for problems we can't solve, people we can't love, habits we can't break, challenges we can't handle, and pasts we can't get past. For all of these and more, there is grace. Please don't wait as long as I did to comprehend that God's grace is enough for anything we face. Our enemy deceives us into believing there is a limit to God's grace, and we have reached it. The apostle Paul had an unidentified struggle he called his "thorn in the flesh" (2 Corinthians 12:7). But when he asked God to get rid of it, the Lord encouraged him with these words: "My grace is sufficient for you" (verse 9).

God's grace is sufficient for any and all situations: when we do the very thing we promised not to do, disappoint people who were counting on us, forget what we should have remembered, say something we shouldn't, habitually arrive late, hurt people we love, and whatever else we can add to the list. No matter what our failures are, we will never live in a place God's grace cannot reach. My favorite grace verse reminds us that our High Priest, Jesus, was tempted just like we are, so He understands our weaknesses even though He didn't sin. Then it continues, "Therefore let us draw near with confidence to the throne of grace, so that we may receive mercy and find *grace* to help in time of need" (Hebrews 4:16, emphasis added).

The consequences of rejecting the truth of God's grace are grave, so we must remind ourselves and the people we care about to make the conscious commitment to hold on to it. Although we can't go backward and have a new start, God's grace lets us leave the past behind. Then His gift of grace enables us to reach forward to a brand-new middle and ending. Paul's words in Philippians 3:13-14 are a good reminder: "One thing I do: forgetting what lies behind and reaching forward to what lies ahead, I press on toward the goal for the prize of the upward call of God in Christ Jesus."

The grace of God empowers us to walk with Him, talk with Him, and live a life that reflects His glory. It infuses us with the energy to do what He calls us to do and to live out His wonderful plan for our lives. We are accepted, forgiven, and empowered by enough grace to also extend it to people in our spheres. Passing out grace like we do tracts on mission trips affords us life-impacting opportunities to influence others.

REFLECTION

Memorize 2 Corinthians 12:9, a short but important reminder that God's grace is sufficient for everything we encounter in life. What do you need His grace for today? Spend a few minutes thanking the Lord for His grace that saved you, and then ask for grace to honor Him in whatever you do. As you unwrap God's gift of grace to you, reflect on the words from "Amazing Grace," written by a former slave-ship owner who repented of his sin and received forgiveness from our gracious God. Read or sing the words below, or listen to a recording of this beautiful hymn.

> *Amazing grace! How sweet the sound*
> *That saved a wretch like me!*
> *I once was lost, but now am found,*
> *Was blind but now I see.*[2]

19

WORSHIP

We watched the long line of solemn-faced worshipers haul a variety of animals to sacrifice to their god, one of 330 million gods in their religion. Walking barefoot, despite the cold, the poorer families carried doves and chickens. By contrast, the wealthy people brought goats. Children held on to their small birds or the hem of their father's garment as they made their way down the hill.

In this rural area, the hill of mud, with a small stream of water near the bottom, served as a temple where the priest blessed the weekly sacrifices. Our national partners explained that each blood sacrifice was offered to gain an answer to prayer or to appease an angry god. But since the people would never

Worship is humbling ourselves

before God because we are

overwhelmed by His love and

grace, so thankful for who He is

and what He has done.

know whether their requests were answered, they trudged back up the hill with the same sad faces. The scene was so upsetting that I wept the first time I witnessed idol worship in one of the countries where Bob and I minister.

We may be too sophisticated in our culture to worship a god requiring the blood of animals. Instead, we worship the idols accepted in our world: personalities, ideas, status, education, popularity, wealth, and whatever you might fill in the blank with. These subtle idols threaten to invade the places in our hearts that belong to God alone.

What is worship? When I began to attend church in college, I was embarrassed to admit that I had no idea what worship was. Then, for a religion class, I read the book of Revelation. I didn't understand it, but for the first time, I experienced worship. Tears filled my eyes as I read this passage:

I heard the voice of many angels around the throne and the living creatures and the elders; and the number of them was myriads of myriads, and thousands of thousands, saying with a loud voice, "Worthy is the Lamb that was slain to receive power and riches and wisdom and might and honor and glory and blessing." And every created thing which is in heaven and on the earth and under the earth and on the sea, and all things in them, I heard saying, "To Him who sits on the throne, and to the Lamb, be blessing and honor and glory and dominion forever and ever." And the four living creatures kept saying, "Amen." And the elders fell down and worshiped.

REVELATION 5:11-14

The term *worship*, as it's used in the Bible, implies bowing. Worship is bowing before God, acknowledging His rightful place in our lives. It involves removing any potential idols, those things that threaten God's rightful place in our hearts. We were made to worship. We either worship God or we worship something He created. Paul warned the Romans not to exchange "the truth of God for a lie" by worshiping and serving "the creature rather than the Creator, who is blessed forever" (Romans 1:25).

Worship is humbling ourselves before God because we are overwhelmed by His love and grace, so thankful for who He is and what He has done. He is a mighty God: holy, loving, just, righteous, true, kind, gracious, infinite, omnipresent, omniscient, and so much more. And He has done mighty works. In the words of Moses, "O Lord GOD, You have begun to show Your servant Your greatness and Your strong hand; for what god is there in heaven or on earth who can do such works and mighty acts as Yours?" (Deuteronomy 3:24). The works of God are too numerous to count. He created the world and every creature, from angels to the ant. Yet His greatest work was not creation but salvation. It took God's fingers to put the moon and stars in space (see Psalm 8:3), but it took His strong arm to send His only Son to die in our place and to raise Him from the dead: "The LORD has bared His holy arm in the sight of all the nations, that all the ends of the earth may see the salvation of our God" (Isaiah 52:10).

As I read the passages above and think more about worship, I am both convicted that I too often neglect this privilege and encouraged that the Lord draws me close. Worship may not begin as a spiritual experience, but it seems to lead to one: a sweet time of fellowship that moves our hearts in the direction of our Savior.

REFLECTION

Take time from your busy schedule to worship the Lord. The Bible encourages us to worship Him in spirit and truth (see John 4:23). Bask in His love for you. Talk to Him, listen to Him, sing to Him. Worship can be corporate, and it can also be a meaningful personal time between your heavenly Father and His grateful child.

20

WHEN I AM AFRAID . . .

"I'M SO AFRAID!" the young woman exclaimed as I sat down next to her on the plane.

"Is this your first time to fly?" I asked.

"Well," she replied, "it's the first time I've flown by myself, and I just left my two little kids. My aunt had an accident."

I had planned to work on the plane, but I quickly realized the Lord had other plans for me.

"Did you know there is a verse in the Bible that reminds us God will help us when we're afraid?" I asked her.

"My mom told me about verses like that, but she passed away. Will you tell me one?" she begged.

At that moment, I was grateful for fearful circumstances I'd experienced through the years. Desperate to memorize applicable Scripture, I packed "fear" verses in my brain like I packed clothes in my suitcase for my trip. I quoted her Isaiah 41:10: "Do not fear, for I am with you; do not anxiously look about you, for I am your God. I will strengthen you, surely I will help you, surely I will uphold you with My righteous right hand."

"Can you tell me more?" my seatmate asked.

"My favorite is Psalm 56:3-4," I shared. "'When I am afraid, I will put my trust in You. In God, whose word I praise, in God I have put my trust. I shall not be afraid. What can mere man do to me?'" I told her the story of our first week in the Philippines, when a robber broke into a room where my children and I were staying while my husband was traveling to another island to secure a home for us.

My seatmate wiped her tears as she listened intently. I had the incredible privilege of watching the power of God's Word envelop her with His peace.

"I think I'll sleep now," she said.

I couldn't help but think of Psalm 4:8: "In peace I will both lie down and sleep, for You alone, O LORD, make me to dwell in safety." After the burglary episode, I put this passage together with Psalm 56:3-4 and sang them every night to my children as long as they allowed me to tuck them into bed.

I no longer sing these verses to my children, but my children sing them to their children. And the result is the same: peace, the absence of fear. Because fears are real and occur daily, I still sing the verses to myself.

As our plane began its descent, my new friend woke up and smiled. "I'm so glad I changed my seat," she said. I had actually changed my seat too. How like the Lord to orchestrate our encounter!

You may not be afraid of flying, but what about the fears of rejection, failure, change, loneliness, disappointing people, losing your job, public speaking, getting old, missing out, job interviews, spiders, car accidents, losing your way, natural disasters, a down economy, or death? The young woman next to me might have assumed that I had it all together and never dealt with fear. But when I sat down next to her on the plane, I feared failing to complete my long to-do list and being inadequate for the challenging event that awaited me.

For all of the above circumstances, the biblical command is clear: "Do not fear!" The psalmist reminds us that when fear creeps in—and it will—we must put our trust in the Lord, who will help us. Prepare and train for fears in the same way you do for a race, a job, or a speech. Exchange fears for peace, like the woman on the plane did. She hugged me as we exited, hesitating to let go. I reminded her that although we were heading in different directions, the Lord would always be with her to give peace and take away fear.

What fear stands between you and peace? The Lord waits to make that incredible trade—our fears for His peace.

REFLECTION

What fears keep you up at night? Memorize a "fear" verse and quote it to yourself as you go to sleep. You might want to add Psalm 4:8 too— the perfect lullaby for all ages. Reread Isaiah 41:10 and think about what it means to be upheld by God's hand. He will never leave you!

21

THE POSSIBLE
IN IMPOSSIBLE

Many things that were impossible when I was young are not only possible today but also commonplace: smartphones and smart watches, e-readers, electric cars, 3D movies, Alexa, and spell-check. Our idea of what seems impossible changes constantly.

God calls us to believe the possible in what seems impossible: to follow Him without knowing the destination, to trust Him with the desires of our hearts, to rely on His plans that don't always make sense to us. Trusting God for the impossible enables us to become less dependent on what others think and more dependent on Him. This is what the Bible calls *faith*.

And Hebrews 11:6 tells us that "without faith, it is impossible to please God" (NIV).

When I was twelve years old, I walked to church with my little sister and responded to the gospel the first time I heard it. I knew nothing about faith, but that day I believed that God had sent His Son, Jesus, to pay for my sins on the cross. I couldn't see Jesus, but I asked Him to be my Savior. With the faith of a child, my eternity was changed—the *possible* in *impossible*. My parents didn't let me return to that church, but God continued to do the impossible in my life as He slowly transformed me.

My husband has an impossible story too. At sixteen, he attended a Christian ski camp because he wanted to see snow. It never snowed, but when he heard that God loved him enough to send Jesus to die for him, he responded to His love.

The faith story Bob and I would write together may seem embellished, made for TV, impossible to believe. We were not likely candidates to do the impossible, but the God we placed our faith in is not limited by personalities or circumstances. By faith, Bob helped start a Christian movement on our college campus. Two years later, as a student, I met him and attended his group's weekly gathering, where I learned more about the Christian life and the Bible. With a little bit of faith, I started a Bible study with the girls who lived around me. Bob is known for his courage, but courage is not my strong suit. I was learning, however, that every time the Lord gave a seemingly impossible assignment to people in the Bible, from Noah to His disciples, He promised, "I will be with you." *Would He be with me too?* I wondered when I invited the girls to join me.

Do you wonder whether God will be with you, should you attempt the impossible? The Bible assures us that He will be with us "always, even to the end of the age" (Matthew 28:20). What impossibility is circling in your mind, causing your heart to beat faster? Is God calling you to go on a mission trip, volunteer at a pregnancy center, share the gospel with a coworker, foster children, repair a damaged relationship, or something else?

When we put our little bit of faith in our big God, He does the impossible. I have a sense of awe when I ponder the impossible transformation God made in my life and in the lives of the girls who joined me in our campus Bible study. Each story is unique, but in the years since college, all of us have counted on the Lord to make the impossible possible. One friend counted on Him to restore a marriage. Another dealt with terminal breast cancer, while another surrendered her fears as she regularly ministered in Cuba. I carried a baby that a doctor warned me to abort—or we would both die. The Christian group Bob helped start is still going strong on that college campus fifty years later. Trusting God to do the impossible has a ripple effect that we will not fully comprehend until heaven, and He alone gets all the glory!

Life is replete with things that seem impossible. Don't let fear, doubt, and insecurity prevent you from trusting God's plan. He won't ask you to do what He asked of me. He has a unique plan for you, and it's an impossible plan too—one that requires faith. But Matthew 19:26 reminds us, "With God all things are possible." And you can be assured that He will be with you every step of the way, backing you up.

Isaiah 42:16 says, "I will lead the blind by ways they have not known, along unfamiliar paths I will guide them; I will turn the darkness into light before them and make the rough places smooth. These are the things I will do; I will not forsake them" (NIV). Our small faith in our mighty God makes the impossible possible.

REFLECTION

Take some time to pray and consider what God might be asking you to do. What seems impossible about it? Write down Matthew 19:26 and Matthew 28:20 to remind yourself that God will never leave you and that all things are possible with Him.

22

THE ACCIDENT

Bob and I had promised our friend that we would attend her daughter's college basketball game, and we enjoyed cheering on the team and seeing our friend. We had taken separate cars, so I ran a few errands after the game and then headed home, grateful that the traffic was not as heavy on Saturday.

In a hurry to get home, I was thankful for a green arrow as I exited off the interstate. The woman driving toward me was in a hurry too. But she was not familiar with the area and commented later that she had been looking for the entrance to the interstate. In her quest to find it, she failed to notice the red traffic light above her and slammed into the front of my car.

As my compact car limped across the road to an elementary

school entrance, my first thought was to thank the Lord. It's not because I had a superspiritual moment. Over many years, however, my brain has been programmed to thank the Lord first. I wasn't "excited thankful" or happy to have been in the accident; I was thankful by faith. My natural reaction to challenging circumstances is frustration, but being thankful for circumstances, no matter what, is my spiritual programming. How could I be thankful when I was just in a car accident? I've had years of training with "In everything give thanks, for this is God's will for [me] in Christ Jesus" (1 Thessalonians 5:18).

Sometimes I get myself in trouble, but other times, like this incident, I have no control over what happens to me. Either way, I have control over my response. Over the years, my responses have probably been wrong more than they have been right, but this time, I quoted my verse immediately while I checked to see if I was bleeding.

Several years earlier, my sons had made certain that my first new car was ultrasafe. Their protective instinct paid off. My car was damaged, but I was okay—just rattled.

The other woman and I checked on each other to make sure we were not hurt. I waited a minute and then said calmly, "You just ran a red light."

"What light?" she responded.

We had both called our husbands, and they showed up

quickly. Her husband talked her into changing her story. He looked at me and stated abruptly, "It's your fault. Even if you had a green light, you should look both ways before you turn!" What could I say to that? I decided to let the police officer handle it.

When he arrived, I started to tell him my side of the story, and he responded, "I don't care!" You can guess how it went from there. Grateful for insurance, I knew there was nothing else Bob and I could do at the moment.

"It's not fair" would have been my response in years past, but as my husband often reminded our family, "Life's not fair!" From the time they were young, we attempted to pass on this bit of wisdom to our kids. I still remember when our four-year-old exclaimed to his toddler brother, who had just skinned his knee trying to keep up, "Life is not fair!" He got the "not fair" part, but we still needed to work on compassion.

So many things happen in life that seem unfair, both on a small and large scale. The Lord has taught me from experience and from His Word that life is not fair, but He can be trusted. Nearly three thousand years ago, King Solomon, the wisest man who ever lived, wrote a book contrasting how unfair our lives can seem at times with the fact that we have an all-wise God, who will one day right every wrong. Solomon writes in Ecclesiastes 8:14, "In this life, good people are often treated as though they were wicked, and wicked people are often treated as though they were good. This is so meaningless!"(NLT). My translation would be, "This is so unfair!" Years before King Solomon, Moses wrote, "[The Lord] is the Rock; his deeds are perfect. Everything he does is just and fair. He is a faithful God who does no wrong; how just and upright he is!" (Deuteronomy 32:4, NLT).

When "accidents" happen over the course of our lives and their outcomes seem unfair, how should we respond? Remember that God can use accidents and other hard circumstances to refine us and prepare us for His purposes and plans. And because we can trust Him to work out every circumstance for good, our response should be one of trust and thanksgiving.

REFLECTION

How do you respond when you feel that something is unfair? Think of an applicable verse you could program into your mind that would help you react with trust and thanksgiving rather than anger and frustration. Write out this verse and place it where you will see it every day.

23

ALL THINGS WORK FOR GOOD–EVEN ACCIDENTS

IN THE PREVIOUS DEVOTION I talked about remembering 1 Thessalonians 5:18 and thanking God in the immediate aftermath of my car accident. But the accident also brought another verse to mind, the first one I programmed into my brain years ago when I started memorizing Scripture: "We know that God causes all things to work together for good to those who love God, to those who are called according to His purpose" (Romans 8:28).

Although the police officer who arrived on the scene of my accident was not interested in the facts of what had happened or the people involved, that situation changed quickly. Within minutes following a call Bob made to a friend, five

Never underestimate

the fact that when we love God

and are called according to

His purpose, He can weave all

things, even the worst things,

together for good.

officers appeared, and they were very interested in both facts and people. The other driver didn't change her story, but the new presiding officer took both our statements and insisted I see a doctor.

The next day, my family began arriving in town for Thanksgiving, so taking time away from them to see a doctor was the last thing I wanted to do. But the same friend Bob had called from the accident scene was insistent that I see a specific doctor, his neighbor.

Grumbling to myself a few days later as I struggled to locate the doctor's office, I forced my brain to switch to Romans 8:28. I couldn't imagine how "all things" in this situation would work out for good, but I knew my responsibility was to love and trust the Lord.

When I arrived at the doctor's office late on the afternoon before Thanksgiving, it was no surprise that I was the only patient.

"Come in," the doctor encouraged me as soon as I arrived.

As I walked into the examining room, he blurted out, "I just finished watching a video of you on YouTube, and you told the audience how they can know Jesus."

I couldn't seem to process his comment quickly enough to respond.

"But first, let's check you out," he said, loud enough that his nurse could hear from the other room.

Under a minute later, he shut the door and was eager to continue the conversation. "Can you explain to me how I can have a relationship with Jesus, like you told those people about?"

Romans 8:28 flashed in my mind. I knew God could work bad things for good, but I guess I didn't expect the purpose to be this obvious. At first I was a little upset that the doctor had seen me speaking on YouTube since I don't post any videos and my contract for speaking events clearly states that no filming is allowed, especially for social media purposes. But then I realized that this doctor had just watched me sharing the gospel, and now he wanted to know more. How could I be upset? I prayed silently for help and then explained the good news of Jesus, with the doctor interrupting occasionally to share why his wife had just left him, taking their daughter with her.

When I asked the doctor whether he had questions, he replied, "Just one. Will you pray with me to ask Jesus to be my Savior?"

"Of course," I responded as I handed him one of the little gospel booklets I always carry. We prayed together and then talked for a minute, and I left with a clean bill of health, eager to join my family.

I walked to my rental car in disbelief. *Did that really just happen?* I felt as dazed as I had been when the woman's car hit mine a few days earlier, and my response was the same: "In everything give thanks; for this is God's will for you in Christ Jesus" (1 Thessalonians 5:18).

No one will believe me, I thought as I left the doctor's office. Maybe you don't as you read this, but it's true—every word of it. Only God can write a story like this one. He used a car accident to direct me to another side of town, to a doctor who was desperate to know Jesus. Wow! Never underestimate the fact that when we love God and are called according to His purpose, He can weave all things, even the worst things, together for good.

REFLECTION

As you think back on your life, can you identify some moments that seemed bad at the time but resulted in something good? How did God work through the difficulty for your good and His glory? Thank Him for His work in the past, and trust Him to do the same in whatever challenges you are facing now. Make sure Romans 8:28 is cemented in your mind, helping you remember to respond in love to the God who loves you, has a purpose for your life, and works *everything* out for your good.

24

THE GREATEST OF ALL

HUMAN NATURE DRAWS US like magnets to admire the "greatest" in any category, including technology, books, movies, and especially people. Our world assesses human greatness on the basis of riches, beauty, power, status, strength, and accomplishments. To earn credibility, we strive to be the "greatest" in our profession, sport, or area of talent.

The Bible also has a "greatest" designation. Although the contest for the title is open to every Christian, limited numbers enter. Why? Because the qualifications are challenging, and the prize won't be awarded here and now—and who wants to wait for recognition?

Can you guess who qualifies to be the greatest? You might think the answer is Christians who have the biggest media platforms or speak to the largest audiences, but instead, it's people like my friend Joy, who brings smiles to critically ill children with her therapy dog and pony. And there's the couple who runs our safe house for rescued girls, the thousands of volunteers at Night to Shine, and the staff and volunteers at our local pregnancy center. My two friends named Sue are too humble to claim "greatness" status. So are Stacey, Jennifer, Jean, Karen, and Brandi, and yet they all work tirelessly in their different areas of ministry to serve others and share God's love. When we get to heaven, we will be surprised by the unknowns who will be summoned to the front of the "greatest of all" line.

Two of Jesus' disciples, James and John, attempted to qualify as the greatest, even asking Jesus whether they could sit in the most important places by His side in heaven. They were stunned when Jesus explained the concept of greatness to them: "Whoever wishes to become great among you shall be your servant; and whoever wishes to be first among you shall be slave of all. For even the Son of Man did not come to be served, but to serve, and to give His life a ransom for many" (Mark 10:43-45).

The disciples didn't anticipate that the road to greatness would be paved with serving, hard work, and humility. Servants don't get to brag about their achievements or seek recognition for their work. Good servants don't even complain. The "greatest of all" example and inspiration for serving is our Savior, who served us with humility: "Have this attitude in yourselves which was also in Christ Jesus, who, although He existed in the form of God, did not regard equality with God a thing to be grasped, but emptied Himself, taking the form of a bond-servant" (Philippians 2:5-7).

Having the spiritual gift of service is not a prerequisite for serving; everyone is called to serve. We learn how to do it from observing servants in action. Serving is not natural to me, but years ago I discovered that in the context of serving, I could have my greatest influence. Like many of us, I would rather be out in front than behind closed doors, but the Lord blessed me with a husband and five children, all of whom needed someone to serve them. He then sent me to an obscure mission field, where my family started multiple ministries in need of servants. When we moved back to the US, there were serving opportunities at church and in the community. Over time, I had to learn not to complain or reject the opportunity when I was called upon to serve.

We taught our kids that serving is the means to greatness: "The greatest among you must be a servant. But those who exalt themselves will be humbled, and those who humble themselves will be exalted" (Matthew 23:11-12, NLT). I put these verses to a catchy tune so we could sing them over and over—and live them out. As we watched Bob serve those who couldn't reciprocate, we followed his lead.

As you read this devotion, does a ministry or a person you could serve come to mind? A family provides a ready-made opportunity. So does a job. Servants bless their homes, offices, schools, neighborhoods, and churches. There are more opportunities to serve than there are servants.

Become a member of the "greatest among us." You may need to wait until heaven to receive your prize, but Jesus Himself will reward you there for your faithful service (see 2 Corinthians 5:10). And He will say to you, "Well done, good and faithful servant; you were faithful over a few things, I will make you ruler over many things. Enter into the joy of your lord" (Matthew 25:21, NKJV).

REFLECTION

Where are you serving already? Where else could you begin to serve? Check on the needs of a homeless shelter, an after-school program, your church nursery, or various other ministries in your community. Wherever you serve, ask God to help you do it with humility and grace. Choose your favorite verse about serving and post it in a prominent place to remind you that God values servants.

25

WARNING SIGNS

ONE NIGHT A FEW MONTHS AGO, my flight home from a speaking event arrived late. Once in my car, tired and eager to get home, I spotted what I assumed to be a new shortcut to the airport exit. I made a quick decision to try it, and a split second later, headlights flashed in my eyes as a car headed straight toward me. By God's grace, I was able to turn around just in time. All the way home, I thanked the Lord for my sovereign rescue.

When I returned from my next trip, Bob was in town to pick me up. As we approached the new road, I spotted an impossible-to-miss "Wrong Way" sign right where I'd turned before. I now have a new appreciation for warning signs! The major interstate running through the middle of our large city is being updated, with confusing new entrances and exits being added regularly, but, thankfully, warning signs seem to be everywhere.

Warning signs are also all over the Bible. Why? So we can avoid a head-on crash into life-altering, messy consequences: broken marriages, estranged friendships, tarnished reputations, foolish choices, financial setbacks, and more. Bob and I were not reared in homes where the Bible was read, but we didn't want that to be true of our home. When our children were young and life was less complicated, we determined to read from Psalms and Proverbs every day at breakfast. Labeled the "Wisdom Book," Proverbs has thirty-one chapters, one for each day of most months.

Solomon, the wisest man who ever lived and the author of Proverbs, described his collected sayings this way: "Their purpose is to teach people to live disciplined and successful lives, to help them do what is right, just, and fair. These proverbs will give insight to the simple, knowledge and discernment to the young" (Proverbs 1:3-4, NLT). Wise warnings about the consequences of our actions, words, and thoughts are packed into each chapter. Although Bob and I must wait until heaven to comprehend the full impact of reading the warning signs from Proverbs to our children day after day, year after year, we've had a few glimpses of their influence.

When one of our daughters was in college, a cute football player expressed interest in meeting her. A few days later, she saw him at a school event she attended with girlfriends. When she witnessed him lose his temper and punch a fellow student, she immediately called to tell me that a giant neon warning sign had flashed in her mind: "Do not associate with a man given to anger; or go with a hot-tempered man" (Proverbs 22:24). As she relayed the incident, I whispered, "Thank You, Lord!" My competitive daughter memorized more proverbs than her siblings in order to earn "Daddy's Dollars" for special privileges, but the long-term worth of knowing the warning signs is priceless.

Bob regularly emphasized the warning signs concerning friendships, including this one: "Walk with the wise and become wise; associate with fools and get in trouble" (Proverbs 13:20, NLT). One son struggled to apply this proverb with a particular friend, but he had heard this warning countless times and eventually made the hard choice to back away. I'm especially thankful for Bob's wisdom to emphasize this verse because sadly, a few years later, the young man died from a drug overdose.

Recently I found my old Bible and opened it to Proverbs. The pages were coffee stained, littered with notes, and partially ripped from the binding. As Bob and I read Proverbs to instruct our kids, this book of countercultural wisdom also warned, convicted, and encouraged me. There are warnings about anger, gossip, greed, boasting, and jealousy, as well as teaching on finances, friendships, purity, self-control, speech, and manners. Character qualities such as kindness, diligence, and compassion are also highlighted. Proverbs provided a full curriculum on wise living, but our family's life-impacting take-away was the tragic warning that Solomon, the wisest man who ever lived, failed to apply God-given wisdom to his own life, and the consequences were grave.

REFLECTION

For the next month, read a chapter from Proverbs each day, and determine to heed the wise warnings. Choose a favorite warning verse to memorize and apply. Type it in your phone or write it on a note card, share it with a family member, or text it to a friend. You may not earn "Daddy's Dollars," but biblical warning signs have great value (see Proverbs 2). As Proverbs 16:16 says, "How much better it is to get wisdom than gold!"

26

FAITHFUL

I USUALLY WHISPER "GOOD MORNING" to the Lord when I wake up. I never wonder whether He's there; He always is. God's faithfulness is as sure as the sun in the sky each morning.

Amid life's distractions, we need to remember God's promise that He will be faithful every day. Years ago, I memorized Bible verses about God's faithfulness and taught them to my children. I encouraged my kids to take the verses with them as they travel through life—so they can recall God's faithfulness when circumstances are hard, when the workload is heavy, or when the pain is intense.

We often pass down family heirlooms to our children, but

even more significant are the spiritual truths we plant in their hearts. One such truth for our family is found in the eight verses of Psalm 121. Shortly after we moved to the Philippines, Bob was away preaching, with no means of communicating with us at home. I clearly recall asking God for a reminder of His faithfulness, as my four young children and I attempted to cope with unfamiliar circumstances. One morning I opened my Bible to this psalm and added a simple tune to help us memorize it. We needed it in our minds so the Holy Spirit could enable us to apply its truths to our lives. Remaining confident of God's faithfulness was essential for all of us!

When my oldest grandchild, Claire, was five, she called with a surprise for me. In her sweet voice, she sang to me the whole psalm, one she called a "Grandma song." I cried tears of joy! She lived on a different mission field than her mother did when she was growing up, but Claire and her family also needed reminders of God's faithfulness:

I will lift up my eyes to the mountains;
From where shall my help come?
My help comes from the LORD,
Who made heaven and earth.
He will not allow your foot to slip;

He who keeps you will not slumber.
Behold, He who keeps Israel
Will neither slumber nor sleep.

The LORD is your keeper;
The LORD is your shade on your right hand.
The sun will not smite you by day,
Nor the moon by night.
The LORD will protect you from all evil;
He will keep your soul.
The LORD will guard your going out and your coming in
From this time forth and forever.

PSALM 121:1-8

Overwhelming challenges can rob us of our hope unless a trustworthy security guard is in place. We have God's personal guarantee that we will find hope when we recall the truth that His love never ceases and His compassion never ends. We'll have hope to believe that when we fail and when people around us fail, God's love and compassion never will. The following verses, written humanly by the Old Testament prophet Jeremiah and supernaturally by the Holy Spirit of God, serve to protect our minds and hearts and assure us of our secure hope:

This I recall to my mind, therefore I have hope. The
LORD's lovingkindnesses indeed never cease, for His
compassions never fail. They are new every morning;
great is your faithfulness.

LAMENTATIONS 3:21-23

God's responsibility is to guarantee His faithful love and
mercy every morning. Our part is to recall this truth to our
minds, especially when our hope begins to waver. The promised
result of remembering these verses is hope. When we possess
hope, it overflows to influence the people in our spheres with
the life-impacting assurance of God's faithfulness.

One person Bob and I can encourage with God's promise
to remain faithful is Ted, a neighbor who handles some of
our farm chores. Even before Bob mentions a task, Ted senses
the need and is on the job. Faithful and kind, Ted closely
resembles the God he serves. Ted counts on God's faithful
mercy as he cares for his dear wife, who suffers from advanced
dementia. We can't predict whether our assignment will be as
challenging as Ted's, but Ted would tell you that God is faithful to extend His love and compassion for every challenge of
every day.

REFLECTION

Spend a few minutes reflecting on God's faithfulness to you during the challenges you face now. It will be worth the time required to cement the truth about God's faithfulness in your mind. Consider memorizing a passage about God's faithfulness, such as Lamentations 3:21-23, in your favorite version of the Bible. Then sing the refrain of this great old hymn about God's faithfulness:

Great is Thy faithfulness! Great is Thy faithfulness!
Morning by morning new mercies I see;
All I have needed Thy hand hath provided—
Great is Thy faithfulness, Lord, unto Me! [3]

Choosing contentment, choice

by choice, may be life's greatest

challenge, but it could also result in

your most important opportunity to

impact our watching world.

27

CHOOSE CONTENTMENT

Shortly after our family returned to America from the mission field, I was asked to speak to a sizable group of women on "The Greatest Lesson I Have Learned." The topic I chose was contentment, but I substituted "am learning" for "have learned," because I knew I hadn't arrived. In fact, I'm still learning!

The word *contentment* often causes eyes to roll and ears to tune out because it's so convicting. I didn't choose to sign up for "contentment class," but I was forced to join a few weeks into my marriage. Bob and I were grateful to find an inexpensive, convenient place to live while we worked and attended grad school. We enjoyed inviting other students to our little apartment for dinner, until one asked, "How can you be content to live in such a tiny apartment?"

How can I be content? I wondered. Do you ask yourself the same question? How can we keep from envying what others have? How do we stop complaining about what we don't have? How do we count our blessings rather than list our wants? How can we be content when we can't even turn on a device without seeing an enticement to covet something we don't own?

The apostle Paul also attended "contentment class" while under house arrest in Rome. In his accelerated classes, 2 Corinthians 12:10 says he learned to be content with weaknesses, insults, distresses, persecution, and difficulties—for the sake of Christ. When I read this verse in those early years, I remember thinking that my small apartment didn't belong in the same category as persecution. But I was in the beginner's class, taking my first steps on the path to learning contentment. The road ahead, however, would include a crash course in challenges not listed on my syllabus.

Why do we need to deal with hard things? Because issues we can't solve in our own strength cause us to "seek the Lord and His strength" (Psalm 105:4). Our young athletes claimed the verse "I can do all things through Christ who strengthens me" (Philippians 4:13, NKJV) for athletic endeavors but later learned they also needed strength to be content with both the wins and the losses of life.

Read what Paul writes immediately before this famous verse:

"I know how to get along with humble means, and I also know how to live in prosperity; in any and every circumstance I have learned the secret of being filled and going hungry, both of having abundance and suffering need" (Philippians 4:12). With this context, we can see that "all things" in verse 13 refers to choosing contentment when we have *a little* or when we have *a lot.* So we remain in contentment class, whether we are looking for a job or celebrating a raise, whether we have outgrown our homes or are moving to our dream houses.

A contented person understands that the things of this world are here when we arrive and are left behind when we exit this life. But in between, we struggle to be satisfied with what we have. Years ago, I thought I had a handle on this until we entertained a number of couples from church, and someone made a joke about the chicken wallpaper border in our kitchen. I laughed with the others, but I struggled to remain content. Although I knew there were more critical financial priorities than new wallpaper, I needed God's strength and grace to choose contentment every time I saw those chickens. My wallpaper didn't need to change as much as I did. I no longer have chickens on my wall, but there is always something I wish I could change about my life. Until I go to heaven, I must keep choosing contentment by faith and not feeling.

Take time to discuss your contentment challenges with

the Lord. Choosing contentment, choice by choice, may be life's greatest challenge, but it could also result in your most important opportunity to impact our watching world. Paul counted on God's strength and grace to choose contentment, and he graduated from his class with honors. He taught young Timothy his secret: When contentment pairs with godliness, the result is "great gain" (see 1 Timothy 6:6). Contentment is the inner peace, assurance, and strength to accept God's plan and provision. When we choose contentment, we have nothing to lose but bitterness and envy, and we have everything to gain: great gain!

REFLECTION

In what areas do you most struggle with contentment? Reread Philippians 4:11-13, and remember that you can do all things through Christ. Write 1 Timothy 6:8 on a note card or type it in your phone as a reminder that "if we have food and covering, with these we shall be content." And it's okay to change the "we" to "I." Ask God for His supernatural strength to choose contentment—choice after choice, day after day.

28

JOY IN THE MORNING

YEARS AGO, A PERSON CLOSE TO ME traded her joy for bitterness when she allowed jealousy to fester until it consumed her, and she was never the same. I wrote the following poem to express my deep sadness for both her loss and mine.

Where did you lose your joy?
Was it left along the way
To where you're going now?
Oh, I hope that you won't stay.

How did you lose your joy?
Did you set it on the shelf,

In a place that's gloomy and gray,
So descriptive of yourself?

Why did you trade your joy
For a self-centered way of life,
Consumed with resentment,
Bitterness, and strife?

Once upon a time,
Not too long ago,
You shared your joy with me,
But where did that joy go?

We're all tempted to trade joy for bitterness when life is hard. But joy can be ours again when we see our challenges through the encouraging lens of Scripture. As David wrote, "Weeping may last for the night, but a shout of joy comes in the morning" (Psalm 30:5).

The storms of life blow in without warning and rob us of our joy. My husband witnessed firsthand the devastation Typhoon Haiyan caused to the Philippine Islands in November 2013. It was one of the largest recorded typhoons to ever hit land, and more than six thousand people died. Two of his national staff were among the million-plus people who lost their homes in a matter of minutes. Only a divine rescue saved their families. Their initial response to losing their homes was sorrow, but the sadness incredibly evolved to supernatural joy. They used their season of grief and loss to share the mercy and compassion of the Lord, and our ministry was blessed to help with disaster relief efforts. Staff member Primo wrote, "Before the typhoon, the village I lived and preached in had a very low response rate to the gospel. Although my family miraculously survived, Typhoon Haiyan destroyed my home and most of the buildings on my island, which looked like a war zone, littered with debris and coconut trees snapped in half. In the storm's aftermath, I was appointed the sole preacher for relief distribution in forty-five villages, and I have already preached in forty of them, to the largest audiences with the highest response rate I have ever seen. I praise the Lord!"

The prophet Habakkuk wrote about similar circumstances:

Though the fig tree should not blossom
And there be no fruit on the vines,
Though the yield of the olive should fail
And the fields provide no food,
Though the flock be cut off from the fold
And there be no cattle in the stalls,
Yet I will exult in the LORD,

I will rejoice in the God of my salvation.
The Lord God is my strength,
And He made my feet like hinds' feet,
And makes me walk on my high places.

HABAKKUK 3:17-19

In this life, we will experience sorrow and loss, challenging people and circumstances, fear of the future and pain from the past. Our enemy comes to steal, kill, and destroy our joy. But by God's grace, even in the midst of heartbreak and disappointment, we can, like Bob's staff and Habakkuk, rejoice in the God of our salvation.

Our joy can also be diminished by less consequential happenings. My daughter Katie called me one Friday night to tell me her dryer had broken—a minor circumstance compared to the impact of the typhoon, but she still had to make a choice about how she would respond. Saturday morning, she woke up her three daughters with the exciting news: "Guess what we get to do today! Hang all of our clothes on the playhouse to dry!" She sent me pictures of smiling girls and a playhouse covered in clothes. Katie chose joy and influenced her daughters to do the same. Joy is a choice we make, morning after morning, when we face a new day with new challenges.

REFLECTION

Take a few minutes to give your disappointments, sorrows, and pains to your heavenly Father, who alone can comfort you. Then ask the Lord to restore your joy, as King David did at the lowest point in his life: "Restore to me the joy of Your salvation" (Psalm 51:12). In order to prepare for "joy robbers," memorize a favorite "joy" verse or one from this devotion, and ask the Lord to enable you to hold on to your joy through whatever you are facing now.

29

THE GOD WHO SEES
OUR PAIN

"God never wastes our pain when it's offered to Him," my daughter Christy encourages hurting women. In the country where Christy's family ministers, many women are devalued and abused and suffer from great trauma. Christy has the privilege to teach these women the life-changing truth that they are deeply loved by a God who sees them. He never overlooks their challenges or bypasses their pain and suffering.

In Genesis, we read about Sarah's maid, Hagar, who ran away to the desert when she was treated harshly by her mistress. The angel of the Lord appeared to Hagar as she was alone and despairing in the wilderness and assured her that it was safe to return. As a servant, Hagar was not considered important and was sometimes treated poorly, but God valued her enough to communicate with her directly. He saw Hagar's pain, and He promised to give her a son and multiply her descendants so that they would be too many to count.

> The angel of the LORD said to her further, "Behold, you are with child, and you will bear a son; and you shall call his name Ishmael, because the LORD has given heed to your affliction."
> GENESIS 16:11

Hagar understood that God cared about her pain, and she called on the name of the Lord who spoke to her, "a God who sees" (Genesis 16:13).

No matter where we live or who we are, God sees us, and He knows about our pain. He comprehends the unexplainable anguish that invades our lives like an intruder bent on stealing valuables—our self-esteem, purity, health, hope, future, and more.

Pain comes in various forms: Physical pain as we fight cancer. Emotional pain as we experience a severed relationship. Financial pain when our position is terminated and bills stack up. Spiritual pain when we question God's love because life is so hard.

Pain zaps our energy and often leads to bitterness and despair. Like a wicked taskmaster, it can enslave us. But God sees us, and He cares. He doesn't waste the pain in our lives. Perhaps our pain will draw us close to Him, keep us from harm, or enable us to encourage others who are suffering. We may not know God's plan until heaven, but we can be assured, as Hagar was, that He sees us.

Psalm 139 encourages us that God sees us every moment of our lives. From the time He formed us in our mother's womb until we see Him face-to-face, we are never out of His sight. There is no place to flee from His presence. God sees us in the dark because it is as bright as the day to Him. He sees us when we wander. He sees every thought, word, and action. He knows our motives and our deepest desires. He is all around us, in front of us, and behind us. His hand is on us. He leads us. He holds us. He searches us and He knows us.

This psalm was especially meaningful to me when we lived on a faraway island and I was pregnant with our youngest child. I had no medical care, because the only doctor available believed my child was not viable. But I knew that God saw me, and He saw my pain. And I offered it to Him. I couldn't see Him, but I sensed His presence in ways I cannot express in words. God sees you too! You may feel as if you are invisible, that no one really sees you or comprehends your pain and despair. When you begin to doubt that God sees you, turn again to Psalm 139 and meditate on the verses that mean the most to you. Our God sees us, knows everything about us, and loves us perfectly!

REFLECTION

How can we navigate the rough seas of pain, loss, rejection, mis-understanding, or heartbreak? Read Genesis 16. Note God's compassion for Hagar and her response: "You are a God who sees" (verse 13). God sees you and me. He knows us completely, and He has compassion for our pain, even when it's self-inflicted. Offer your pain to Him, knowing that He can use it for good in your life. We can trust the God who sees us.

ENTANGLED

THERE ARE SOME QUESTIONS I would like answered. Can anyone tell me why my favorite necklace, which I always place carefully in my jewelry box, somehow becomes entangled with other jewelry? How does my dress hanger get tangled with a skirt hanger, wrinkling both pieces of clothing and trying my patience as I attempt to separate the two? And let's not even discuss kites intertwining with one another as they fly high overhead, sometimes causing both to plummet to the ground. Our family gave up on flying kites long ago. Too much entangling!

The Bible also deals with entangling, but unlike the examples above, the culprit is identified. You probably already know what it is, but like me, perhaps you'd rather not deal with this topic. The race of life is at stake, however, so we must face the reality of deceptive, entangling, life-ruining *sin*! Our ultimate goal is to run our races in such a way that we will win (see 1 Corinthians 9:24), and that's not possible if we're perpetually stuck in sin. The sin in our lives entangles us, slows us down, and eventually halts our races altogether. Our sin is the focus of the familiar rhyme I taught my kids: "Oh, what a tangled web we weave, when first we practice to deceive."

Why was this devotion low on my list of possible subjects? Because I don't want to dwell on entangling sin. Who does? But we need to if we are people who choose to run life's race free of sin's weight and distractions. Our enemy lurks over runners' shoulders, speaking deceptive lies in our ears. He knows the weaknesses that can entangle us, slow us down, and even halt our races. However, we also have a whole cloud of witnesses serving as examples to follow, people who ran the race before us and are cheering us on. Hebrews 12:1 tells us, "Since we have so great a cloud of witnesses surrounding us, let us also lay aside every encumbrance and the sin which so easily entangles us, and let us run with endurance the race that is set before us."

How are these witnesses involved in our races? The one thing they all have in common is their faith. One of my favorite chapters in the Bible is Hebrews 11, which briefly recounts the stories of many biblical figures who lived by faith—Noah, Abraham, Sarah, Isaac, Jacob, Moses, and others. No matter how many times you've read this familiar passage, you'll be encouraged to read again how these men and women tied together their faith and their walk with God. Their stories remind us that we need to persevere to the finish line, getting rid of anything that slows us down. Faith enables us to confess whatever entangles us and then trust the Lord to forgive our sins.

Just as jewelry, hangers, and kites are easily tangled, Hebrews 12:1 states that sin also "easily" entangles us. For a season, I was entangled with thoughts I shouldn't think, which evolved into actions I shouldn't do and words I shouldn't say. I attempted to justify my slowdown by calling sin another name. Maybe I fooled others, but I didn't fool the Lord.

Why would I choose to stay in a tangled, miserable state? I'm not really sure why anyone makes that choice when we have another option: coming to the God who loves us and stands ready to forgive us and untangle our messes.

Finally one day I called my sin what it was: sin! By faith I confessed it, and by faith I asked for help to lay down the heavy burden and untangle my wrong thinking. What a relief! I also put in place a time in my schedule for regular confession. I recommend this for everyone, because we all get entangled by sin. As hard as it is to admit, there is always a word, a thought, or an action to confess. But by faith we're forgiven when we confess that specific sin. First John 1:9 tells us that "if we confess our sins, He is faithful and righteous to forgive us our sins and to cleanse us from all unrighteousness."

Once we're no longer entangled by sin, we get back in the race—fixing our eyes on Jesus with a clear, untangled conscience—until the next time we sin. There will always be a next time for us while we're on earth, but someday we will go to heaven and meet Him there—our Savior, the One who died to free us forever from the sin that entangles us.

REFLECTION

Read Hebrews 11 and the first three verses of Hebrews 12. Then ask the Lord to help you identify sins that cause you to become entangled. Confess them and thank the Lord for His forgiveness. Ask Him for grace to keep your eyes on Him and run your race with endurance.

31

A LIFE OF PURPOSE

Last Mother's Day, my sweet, creative granddaughter Abby made me a pretty blue stand-alone *P* for *Pam*.

"But, Grandma," she explained, "*P* also stands for *purpose*." She pointed to the statement she had written with a marker on the *P*: "The purpose of life is a life of purpose." Quite profound for a twelve-year-old!

Do you have a purpose? Purpose gives our lives meaning, a reason to wake up in the morning and keep going despite challenges. Some people find the perfect Scripture verse to define their purpose, while others have more than one purpose. There isn't a one-size-fits-all approach. Purpose involves our natural abilities, spiritual gifts, creativity, and season in life, and our purpose can change over time.

My husband is sure of his purpose. Since I first met Bob in college, he has been passionate about getting the gospel to the lost. Those who know him well have no doubt about his purpose, one that keeps him keeping on despite the pain of Parkinson's.

When our son Peter was in college, he echoed his dad's purpose to impact people with the gospel. He intentionally engaged new students, inviting them to join him in activities like Frisbee toss and, later, Bible studies and Christian gatherings. Peter taught campus Bible studies and served two years after graduation on a campus ministry staff. His dual purpose in college resulted in both an engineering degree and the transformation of many students' lives through the gospel.

My purpose hasn't always been quite as clear as my husband's. When I was homeschooling five children on the mission field, my multiple purposes were right in front of me and hard to ignore, and I had little time to deviate from that calling. My family has been an all-consuming purpose, one I am so thankful for. Over the years, my responsibilities shifted as my children grew up, and now God has given me a new sense of purpose through different ministry opportunities. Your purpose might be obvious, like Bob's, or less clear and changing over time, like mine. We all have a variety of responsibilities and occupations that require our time and attention.

Although my friend Jordan has been offered more prestigious jobs, she chooses to serve in one that aligns with her purpose to demonstrate the love of Christ through her varied efforts. Lorie and Sue both teach God's Word to children, who respond to my friends' ability to communicate truth on their level. Tiffany is young and Dottie is retired, but both share the purpose of meeting the practical needs of people in their families, churches, and communities. Whitney, my literary agent, and Katie, my speaker's agent, are both cheerful, energetic working moms. Their jobs provide purpose for them as they use their people skills and discernment to schedule impactful writing and speaking opportunities for their clients—including me, whose purpose is to encourage women by sharing biblical truth and relatable stories.

It's never too late to discover your purpose. When my mother turned seventy, she lamented that she had no purpose, but my two daughters and I encouraged her that God can give us purpose at any age. We made specific suggestions that connected Mom's abilities and passions with her current activities, and she soon became chaplain of her women's club and invited her friends to join her as she ministered to seamen who were docked in their town. Most were foreigners who were receptive to gospel booklets and homemade cookies. Mom also joined a group that made items to raise money for women dealing with cancer.

Purpose enriched her life and the lives of those she impacted until she left us for heaven at age eighty-six.

My passion is encouraging others, but what is yours? The Lord gives us special abilities to use for building others up. We all have different gifts and purposes, and the beauty is that they all work together in God's larger purpose of redemption. As Ephesians 4:16 says, "The whole body, being fitted and held together by what every joint supplies, according to the proper working of each individual part, causes the growth of the body for the building up of itself in love." It's not a pride thing; it's a service thing. Only God could put a plan in place for us to use our gifts to bless others. In return, we are also blessed!

REFLECTION

What do you dream about? What do you do well that blesses others? What motivates you and makes you smile? How do your friends describe you? As you seek to discover your purpose, you will find that usually your spiritual gift is involved: your God-given ability to teach, serve, give, encourage, evangelize, help, and more. Our purpose really is to live a life of purpose! Review the passages on spiritual gifts (especially Romans 12 and 1 Corinthians 12) and ask the Lord to enable you to use the gifts He has given you to invest in the lives of others who need what you have to offer.

32

ADEQUACY FOR TODAY

I WOKE UP MUCH TOO EARLY THAT MORNING, so perhaps my foggy brain is to blame for my sitting in the wrong seat on the plane. The rightful ticket holder looked at me as if I couldn't count, shrugged his shoulders, and sat in my assigned seat. I offered to switch, but his new seat was actually closer to the front of the plane, so he chose martyrdom.

My seatmate—the one who wasn't supposed to be my seatmate—was pleasant. I don't remember how our conversation started, but I remember we didn't want it to end. It evolved from trivial topics to critical ones, from the product responsible for her long eyelashes to the challenges of her blended family.

Is it possible that the Lord woke me up very early that day because I needed more time with Him—not just because I was desperate for adequacy for my speaking event later that evening, but also because I needed His adequacy to minister to the woman sitting beside me on the plane?

Early that morning, I had cried out to the Lord for help to deal with the difficult event coordinator for my challenging event that night and the following day. I'd read some passages in the Bible, and they pointed me to the answer—love. I needed to love others just as God loves me. Of course, I needed the Spirit of God to enable me to love like that.

I shouldn't have been surprised when my seatmate asked for advice in dealing with her blended family. I knew just what to say. "The key is love, unconditional love," I replied. I then shared that the Lord had shown me the answer to her question earlier that day when He had answered mine. I needed her to know that I was just as desperate for God's adequacy as she was.

Both of us had to drop the conditions we'd put on our love. In other words, we needed to love hard-to-love people the way God loves us. We're called to love others unconditionally, with no strings attached. My new friend got it! We talked for the rest of the flight about what that would look like and how impossible it would be to love like this in our own strength. We hugged as we parted, knowing we might not see each other again before heaven. Neither of us had any doubt that our seating mix-up was a setup from the Lord.

Do you ever feel inadequate for the challenges you face daily? I sure do. Put simply, I'm inadequate to deal with the people and responsibilities God has put in my life. I know the Source for all that I need, yet sometimes I choose my own version of adequacy; my limited wisdom instead of the all-wise God's; my good plan instead of God's best plan; my imperfect words instead of the Holy Spirit's grace-filled speech. What am I thinking? On my own, it's impossible for me to be an adequate wife, mom, or friend to the woman sitting next to me on the plane. My adequacy and yours comes from the Lord, and He alone will make us sufficient for everything we encounter in life.

Second Corinthians 3:4-5 tells us, "Such confidence we have through Christ toward God. Not that we are adequate in ourselves to consider anything as coming from ourselves, but our adequacy is from God." I'm glad I chose God's adequacy that day on the plane.

My dear friend Brenda also needs His adequacy to live without Joe, who went to heaven ahead of her. Jan depends on Him for her new role as a single mom. Christine needs His grace as she juggles multiple jobs and ministry. Both Kelly and Karen count on His adequate wisdom each week as they teach multiple Bible studies. My sweet daughter-in-law Casey starts her day before the sun is up to have much-needed time with her Savior, who makes her adequate as a wife and a mom to three kids under five. What do you need adequacy for today?

REFLECTION

Do you feel inadequate to deal with the people and responsibilities in your life? Meditate on 2 Corinthians 3:4-5 this week, and work to memorize this short passage as a reminder that the Lord can make you adequate for everything you face.

33

ALONE AND MISUNDERSTOOD

You MAY LIVE IN A HOUSE full of people or work in a crowded office, and yet I imagine you sometimes feel alone, misunderstood, overlooked, or rejected. I know I do. Friends and family are often too immersed in their own issues to notice ours. Criticism and condemnation are far more prevalent in our world than concern and compassion. Who cares about us, anyway? We already know the answer in our brains, but the reality that God cares needs to make a home in our hearts.

We know from Scripture that our enemy can't win in the end, but he will go to great lengths to ruin the here and now by making us feel hurt and alone. He knows we may struggle to make a positive impact on others when we have wounds that require healing and hearts that need mending.

In the midst of a busy season, surrounded by people, I was wounded when I was unjustly accused. I felt so alone and misunderstood. Then I had a flashback to my first job after college—working in public relations for a bank. A new manager was hired to replace one convicted of embezzlement, and the environment became oppressive because the employees were treated as if we were guilty too. One day I unknowingly helped a prominent customer suspected of participating in the conspiracy. When I was questioned about my involvement, my efforts to be helpful were misinterpreted. I felt so alone!

What about you? Have your motives been misinterpreted, your words misconstrued, your efforts misread? Has your sincerity been doubted? This time, the only thing that spared me from throwing a pity party was remembering that I could choose God's grace over Satan's tricks. Jesus stood alone and rejected so that you and I would not ever need to handle life on our own. Even His Father was forced to turn His back while His innocent Son died on a wooden cross between two thieves. Jesus, the Son of God, cried out, "My God, My God, why have You forsaken Me?" (Mark 15:34). Surely the One who experienced this complete abandonment comprehends our pain and hears our silent cries when we feel rejected and alone.

One day—when, no one knows—Jesus will return to set the record straight. Until that time, He will continue to be misunderstood and rejected by some of the very people He gave His life to save. So how do we deal with similar emotional pain when others turn against us or think badly of us? We follow Jesus' example and trade human rejection for God's acceptance. Is this process of exchanging our hurts for His healing really necessary? It is, if the goal is freedom, peace, spiritual growth—and opportunities to comfort others like He comforted us. When we don't go through this process, the blaming and bitterness that result from taking "into account a wrong suffered" (1 Corinthians 13:5) put us in the same "guilty" category as our oppressors, even when the charges against us are invalid.

My recent experience reveals the ripple effects of God's unmistakable compassion. When I brought Him my pain of rejection and misunderstanding, I experienced His divine comfort. That led to not just one but three opportunities to demonstrate the same compassion to others later that evening. Although I was not in a mood for celebration, Bob and I kept our commitment to attend the birthday party of a close friend. I arrived with a heart supernaturally softened by God's comfort and made ready to care about the challenging circumstances of two guests who didn't yet know my loving Savior. God had comforted me so I could, in turn, comfort them. Then, as I was leaving the party, I received a text from another friend with an urgent need to be comforted. I doubt it was a coincidence!

Does your heart ache? Are you dealing with painful emotions that you can't share with anyone? Run straight to the Lord, who offers comfort for every distress. Then be ready to deliver His unmistakable comfort to hurting people along the way. God gives us the amazing privilege of comforting others with the same comfort we have received from Him.

> Blessed be the God and Father of our Lord Jesus Christ,
> the Father of mercies and God of all comfort, who
> comforts us in all our affliction so that we will be able
> to comfort those who are in any affliction with the
> comfort with which we ourselves are comforted by God.
>
> 2 CORINTHIANS 1:3-4

REFLECTION

Think about a time when you felt misunderstood or unjustly accused. Meditate on the passage above, and then turn to God with your hurt and thank Him that He understands. How can your past experiences help you to share compassion and understanding with those around you who may be hurting?

34

FACING FAILURE

Bob and I had the unusual opportunity to speak on the subject of failure at a charity fundraiser. Although it's not a typical speaking topic, failure is one thing we all have in common. Just reading the word may bring up unpleasant videos on the screens of our minds. We've all seen those sad movies and prefer not to watch the reruns. The great movies are the ones that show the main characters falling down in failure but getting up again as overcomers.

Countless examples of failure fill our history books. It's said that Thomas Edison had a thousand failed experiments in his quest to invent the light bulb, but he persevered. Thanks to his continued efforts, my light overhead enables me to see what I type. Abraham Lincoln lost several elections before he won the presidency and led the country through a civil war.

The Bible also contains stories of failure. Moses was guilty of murder and ran away to tend sheep for forty years, until God called him to lead all two million of His people out of Egypt. When Jesus was arrested, Peter denied knowing Him three times and was devastated by his failure. But after the Resurrection, Peter became a fearless preacher of the gospel and was willing to die a martyr's death.

The apostle Paul led the persecution of Christians in the earliest days of the church. After Jesus appeared to him on the road to Damascus, however, he became a world-class missionary, wrote much of the New Testament, and willingly suffered for his faith. It was this miraculous conversion that enabled him to preach "that Christ Jesus came into the world to save sinners, among whom I am foremost of all" (1 Timothy 1:15).

All of the above were overcomers because they didn't let their failures define them. They didn't allow failure to keep them from taking risks. Has the Lord put something on your heart to do, but you fear failure? Maybe it has to do with your job, your marriage, parenting, an athletic competition, an elected office, or a mission trip. I vividly remember years ago when the Lord impressed on me something I needed to do, but a person I respected warned me of certain failure. With my husband's encouragement and prayers, I took the risk anyway. I look back in gratitude for what God did as I trusted Him for the assignment He had given me.

As a mom, I also had to trust God for wisdom to prepare my kids for both success and failure. Long before my boys played ball games that are watched on highlight reels, they needed to learn to face failure. And our girls, sweet as they are, would fail too. Because we have all faced failure, we are qualified to teach our kids how to deal with losing while they are young, when the loss is forgotten by the time the last pieces of ice in their snow cones are slurped. Later, as losses yield greater consequences, so does the determination to face failure and not give up.

Such lessons came in handy when our son Robby was privileged to play for the high school state championships in both football and baseball, and his team lost both. Our son Timmy had lost games, too, but his goal his junior year in college was for his football team to have an undefeated season. They lost one game by one point.

After Timmy's loss, Bob and I had a few minutes to pray with him before he addressed the media. He apologized to the fans in what is now known as "The Promise," a brief, humble, passionate speech that served as motivation for his team to win the rest of their games that year, including the National Championship. "The Promise" has received a lot of recognition in the years since it was made and is now engraved on the wall of the sports complex at his university.

We can make a promise too—a promise to ourselves: When we fail, we will get up again by God's grace. We will do what we know God has called us to do, and we will not give up on responsibilities, people, or life. We may lose by a point or miss success by a mile, but we can be overcomers. God's Word says so: "This is the victory that has overcome the world—our faith" (1 John 5:4).

REFLECTION

Reflect on your experiences of failure. How have they prevented you from doing what God has called you to do? Read Psalm 73 and pause to meditate on verse 26: "My flesh and my heart may fail, but God is the strength of my heart and my portion forever." Instead of being paralyzed by past failures, we can, by God's grace, commit to being overcomers and getting back up when we fail. Proverbs 24:16 reminds us that "a righteous man falls seven times, and rises again."

35

CAN I TRUST GOD?

WE HAD FINALLY ARRIVED! Bob and I had both sensed God calling us to be missionaries in the Philippines, and after months of preparation, we moved across the world with our four young children to our new country. At last we were in the place God had called us to go.

After a few weeks in Manila, we moved to the island of Mindanao. A few days later, once we were settled in the home of our kind Filipino friends, Bob had to leave us to renew our visas on another island. Trusting God for our family's needs had become part of life, but I still wasn't prepared for the parade of critters that joined us in our temporary home. The cold bucket baths took getting used to, and so did the food. We were excited

Our enemy deceives us into believing that challenging circumstances mean God hates us. It's just the opposite! God loves us, and He is with us every step of the way through our trials.

about fish patties until my daughter pointed out that the black dots resembling pepper were actually the eyes of tiny whole fish.

I was tempted to doubt God like the Israelites did when they finally saw the land He had promised them. Convinced that they would be conquered by the people who lived there, the Israelites cried, "Because the LORD hates us, He has brought us out of the land of Egypt to deliver us into the hand of the Amorites to destroy us" (Deuteronomy 1:27). Our enemy deceives us into believing that challenging circumstances mean God hates us. It's just the opposite! God loves us, and He is with us every step of the way through our trials, even if we step over a strange critter or two.

Amid odd noises, smells, and sights during those weeks when we waited for Bob to return, I watched movies on the screen of my mind—reruns of God's countless demonstrations of faithfulness to our family through the years. The Israelites had a backlog of movies too. In one of them, God parted the Red Sea so they could cross safely while their enemies drowned. Surely that movie won the Academy Award! Yet the people still doubted God when He didn't include their favorite appetizer on the menu.

I knew that if I expressed doubt and disappointment in God's plan to my impressionable children and our gracious hosts, my response would be interpreted as a lack of faith:

"She did not trust in the Lord, she did not draw near to her God" (Zephaniah 3:2). I sensed that this moment of decision was big. So much was at stake. One day I cried out for grace and made the choice to trust God by faith, not because of what I could see or how I felt. I couldn't see the plan, and I sure felt out of place, but I had instant peace. Our circumstances hadn't changed, but that evening, for the first time since we'd arrived, I lay down and slept peacefully, with only a minor concern about critters. I sang Psalm 4:8, which I had put to a tune a few weeks earlier, after the robbery episode: "In peace I will both lie down and sleep, for You alone, O Lord, make me to dwell in safety."

God had us on the straight path of His plan—one that included peace and protection despite all of its seeming twists and turns. We continued to cling to a favorite family verse: "Trust in the Lord with all your heart and do not lean on your own understanding. In all your ways acknowledge Him, and He will make your paths straight" (Proverbs 3:5-6). We can't lean on our own understanding, because the Christian life often makes no sense to us. We stake both our present and future on a God we cannot see.

The truth is, faith isn't a natural response to questionable circumstances. Doubt, fear, and discontent are natural. But faith in the reality of an unseen, sovereign God is what equips us to walk with Him, and our faith is what pleases God (see Hebrews 11:6). Only God's grace can enable ordinary women like us to choose extraordinary faith.

What are you facing that you wouldn't have to deal with if you were in charge? No matter what life looks like from your perspective, God is still in control. He's got it, whatever "it" is: living within your means, changing jobs, major surgery, an upcoming move, or anything else you're facing.

In Deuteronomy 1, Moses encourages the Israelites that God carries His children when they are too weary for the journey, and He goes before them to lead the way (see verses 30-31). You and I need that reminder too. We can make the choice to trust our faithful God!

REFLECTION

What circumstances in your life make you doubt God's presence or His goodness? Think back on your life and choose some "movies" of God's past faithfulness that you can watch over and over to remind yourself that He is good and trustworthy. Review Proverbs 3:5-6 to help you remember that God can be trusted. If you haven't already memorized these key verses, take time to go over them this week so you can take them with you wherever you go.

36

MY TIME IN GOD'S HANDS

I'M SO TIME CONSCIOUS! I check my watch regularly, carry a cute planner in my purse, enter dates on my phone's calendar app, and place calendars throughout our home. I write lists for today, tomorrow, and next week. I commit each day to the Lord, but remaining flexible is a challenge. My daughter Christy reminds me to write my plans in pencil—because plans are subject to change.

I plan because I want my time to count, and you do too. Even if you don't make lists, you have goals and priorities—and that's a good thing. Scripture urges us to use our time on earth well: Paul encouraged the Ephesians to be wise and make the most of their time (see Ephesians 5:15-16). And in Psalm 90,

Moses reminds us to seek God's help to "number our days"—to recognize how short our lives really are—and present to Him a heart of wisdom (see Psalm 90:12).

I'm grateful the Lord invites people like me, who get sidetracked with our own plans, to come to Him for daily wisdom. He promises to give it to us generously. God has the best plans, but I'm not privy to them unless I come to Him. Coming to Him throughout the day is the best use of my time.

God's plans overruled mine when I sent my friend Joanie a birthday card a few years ago. One day she called me in tears to tell me that although my card was postmarked 9-27-17, she had received it a year and a half later, on 5-2-19. My note included a message of hope that she desperately needed the day the card arrived. God's plan, not mine!

I was busy making plans two years ago when the Lord interrupted them. For nearly a year, I periodically blacked out without warning. Twice I blacked out in the shower. The first time, I hit the back of my head, and although I was left with a huge bump, my hair covered the evidence. The next time, however, I fell on my face and looked as if I had been in a fight and lost. Not even sunglasses could hide the conspicuous effects of the fall. My vanity hurt as much as my black eyes.

When it became harder to climb stairs and walk through airports, I decided it was time to seek medical attention. My close friend and internist prays for wisdom about her patients. She talked to the Lord about my health and discerned that I had a heart issue. Since the results of my heart tests were near perfect, no cardiologist believed that was possible. But my friend persisted, and a recorder was placed under my skin to take pictures of my heart when I blacked out.

As I traveled to my next speaking event, I prayed, "When I black out, Lord, please don't let me be injured again." That evening I blacked out and fell into a pile of clothes I was unpacking in the hotel. I spoke the next day and then flew home. Monday morning I called to find out about the recorder results. No one had checked. Just minutes later, after doctors looked at the pictures, I was scheduled for emergency surgery the next day.

In God's timing, my husband was on his thirty-hour trip home from the Philippines. He was with me when I woke up with my new pacemaker, which monitors my heart's electrical system. Just in time! My heart had been stopping, and only God's grace started it again. I'm reminded that "God is greater than our hearts and knows all things" (1 John 3:20).

As I dealt with this life-and-death issue, "a time to be born, and a time to die" (Ecclesiastes 3:2, NKJV) became more of a reality. I began to grasp that my time on earth has limits. If we know Jesus as our Savior, we will live forever with Him, but our time here will end one day. We know the date of our birthdays, but only God knows the day of our funeral. In between birth and death, we can aspire to make our time count. We can prepare now for eternity. An eternal perspective motivates us to share Christ with an unsaved friend, tell family and friends how much we love them, invest in causes with eternal values, settle accounts, and write that note or make that call.

Through it all, we trust God's plans for us. "As for me, I trust in You, O LORD, I say, 'You are my God.' My times are in Your hand" (Psalm 31:14-15).

REFLECTION

As you make plans today, reread Psalm 31:14-15 and remind yourself that God is ultimately in control. Release your plans to Him, and ask for the grace to use your remaining time well, for His glory.

37

GRACIOUS SPEECH

WHILE RUSHING TO CHANGE PLANES in a large airport, I heard a woman call my name. I didn't recognize her, but I slowed my pace and smiled.

"I heard you wrote a book," she said, loud enough for other passengers to hear. "But," she continued, "I know you didn't really write it. Everyone today has a writer."

Her words stunned me, but I was too out of breath from running to catch my plane to respond, and my sole focus was making my connecting flight to the city where I would speak later that evening. I was both relieved to be in the boarding line and thankful for God's grace, which prevented me from responding to unedifying words with unedifying words. Waving to the woman who spoke to me, I boarded last with my carry-on bag and the perfect example of "un-gracious" speech.

The first two Scripture verses I memorized as a young mom were both about gracious speech: "Let no unwholesome word proceed from your mouth, but only such a word as is good for edification according to the need of the moment, so that it will give grace to those who hear" (Ephesians 4:29) and "Let your speech always be with grace, as though seasoned with salt, so that you will know how you should respond to each person" (Colossians 4:6). As a wife and a mother of five, I had countless opportunities to apply these verses. After I had my first child, my sin nature was quickly revealed in my speech, and I began to pray daily for God's grace to sprinkle my speech with love like I sprinkled salt on the food I served my family.

My children no longer live at home, but I still pray these verses daily, because "death and life are in the power of the tongue" (Proverbs 18:21). Our world is desperate for life-giving speech, and those of us who know the Lord are the best equipped to respond to each person we encounter with love and grace.

My mother never recovered from hurtful words spoken to her by her family during her childhood and later as she entered college. Although she excelled in all but one class, her family's certainty that she would fail eventually led Mom to drop out. Job expressed similar pain inflicted by his so-called friends when he was suffering with grief and loss: "How long will you torment me and crush me with words?" (Job 19:2). King Solomon compared harsh words to the thrusts of a sword (see Proverbs 12:18). A few swipes of a sword can do long-term damage to impressionable children, marriages, churches, and friendships. But the strongest warning about our speech is from Jesus: "I tell you that every careless word that people speak, they shall give an accounting for it in the day of judgment" (Matthew 12:36).

Positive words, by contrast, have the power to inspire, motivate, heal, teach, reprove, encourage, love, evangelize, and more. Memorize your favorite "speech verses," or take them with you on a note card to apply as needed as you go through your day. Watch the atmosphere change as you sprinkle encouraging words at the grocery store, office, and gym; at church, in your neighborhood, and especially in your home.

Written words also have the power to build up or tear down. A few months ago, I walked into a restaurant and an implausible God story. The sweet girl I was meeting there has a huge heart to use her support animals to lift the spirits of sick kids at the local children's hospital; she even has degrees and training in this area. Years ago, when our family visited a critically ill child there, I learned about this woman's impact, and I wrote a note to thank her. We exchanged a few Christmas cards over the years, but a few months ago, I sensed the Lord prompting me to invite her to lunch. As we met for the first time, I clung to every word of her fascinating life story.

"I want to show you something," she said as she pulled out a wrinkled paper. "I've kept the note you wrote me in my Bible for the last fourteen years," she explained, handing it to me to see. "The words you wrote encouraged me to keep on serving the kids."

I held back tears until I closed my car door; then I wept all the way home. They were just words that God had prompted me to write on a card, but He used them powerfully because He knew my friend's challenges and her need for encouragement.

Do you wonder whether the small things we do in life really matter? The smiles, the notes, the kind words? I believe they do. How will the positive words you speak, text, or write today impact others? Make the conscious effort to sprinkle gracious words generously!

REFLECTION

In what situations are you most likely to use ungracious words? Memorize one of the many verses on speech that you can apply to those circumstances. Then ask God for the self-control to choose your words wisely today, that they may benefit those who hear them.

38

LOST AND FOUND!

WHEN BOB PROPOSED TO ME, he had just graduated from college. He had saved money from side jobs to buy me an engagement ring, which I loved. Then, years later, one of the prongs broke, and my original diamond was lost. I remember vividly how I cried over my loss. Life goes on, though, and I moved on—until one day when some stranger in a mall, seeing no ring on my finger, asked for my number. After that incident, I bought a cheap fake diamond ring. It wasn't funny at the time. It's so funny now, though!

Bob's aunt was the one who was most concerned about my lost diamond. She had suffered real loss when she was unable to have children, and in a generous gesture to assure her of his love, her husband bought her a beautiful diamond ring. In her later years, as a widow with increasing dementia, she chose to give her ring to me, and she called a family search party because she couldn't remember where she had put it. After hours of searching, one of the cousins found it hidden under her bed, amid piles of clutter. Everyone rejoiced!

Searching is worth the time and effort when what we're seeking is valuable. In Luke 15, Jesus tells three stories about searching for things that were lost. In the first, although the shepherd owned a hundred sheep, each one had value to him. He left ninety-nine in open pasture to search for one who was lost. When he returned with it on his shoulders, everyone rejoiced. Another story describes a woman who had ten silver coins. When she lost one, she searched tirelessly until she found it. Then all her friends and neighbors were invited to rejoice with her. The story most of us recall is that of the Prodigal Son, who left home and squandered his inheritance. The father had two sons, yet when the one wayward son returned home, his father held a great celebration.

My husband is burdened for the "one." When he learned there were small islands in the Philippines whose inhabitants never leave, he realized these people would not be saved if someone didn't come to their islands to preach the gospel. So he added a boat and crew to his evangelistic ministry. Why does he care about a few lost people on hard-to-get-to islands? Because God cares about the "one" who is lost. This is clear from Jesus' own explanation of His purpose: "The Son of Man has come to seek and to save that which was lost" (Luke 19:10).

Individuals are important to God. He sees the one employee in your office who needs someone to explain the gospel to her, the one neighbor, teacher in your child's school, friend from high school, or quirky relative who needs to hear the Good News.

A few years ago, I had an opportunity to share with the "one." I had known her in high school and college, but we eventually followed different paths, and she transferred after our freshman year. We hadn't spoken in forty years when I learned through a dear mutual friend that she was dying of cancer and had asked to see me. But she lived hours away, and my schedule was full.

Yet if I didn't go, who would tell her that God loves her? If she were the only person on earth, God still would have sacrificed His one and only Son for her. I decided to drive the four hours to her home, and my friend agreed to come with me. We shared the Good News with my old friend, and I had the joy of praying with and for her. She died shortly after our visit, but I look forward to spending eternity with her. It was so worth our efforts for the "one."

There was a time when you and I were the lost ones, and

there was great rejoicing in heaven when we were found. Thank the Lord now for God's amazing grace that sought us when we were lost and saved us for all eternity!

REFLECTION

Perhaps a name or a face came to mind as you read this devotion. Pray for that person today, and ask the Lord to give you a heart to care about each "one" who is lost and desperately needs to be found. Prepare now to share the gospel when you have the opportunity. Memorize some key verses, and carry your favorite gospel tract in your purse. So much is at stake!

39

THE GIFT
THAT KEEPS GIVING

Although we hate to admit it, most of us recycle gifts. It makes sense to pass on a gift that could benefit someone in need. Spiritual encouragement is such a gift. When we experience the love and grace of God, we're inspired to "re-gift" the blessing.

I can't recall that anyone ever offered me spiritual encouragement when I was a young Christian. No one reminded me of God's love and my identity in Him, challenged me to grow in my faith, held me accountable to read my Bible and spend time with the Lord daily, or motivated me to share the Good News with others. Then, at the beginning of my sophomore year in college, I attended my first Christian gathering, part of the group Bob started on our campus. To my surprise, I was presented with the priceless gift of spiritual encouragement. I marveled at the obvious display of love for the Lord and for every variety of college kid, even newcomers like me. I returned to the sorority house where I lived, compelled to encourage a few interested girls with the truths I'd just learned.

We met together to study the Bible and encourage each other, and over time, God began to change us. I can't take credit. I only shared the gift, but God multiplied my feeble efforts. And for the first time, I began to comprehend our God-given potential for influence. The result was inexpressible joy, purpose, and a passion to encourage others. Last week, one of my dearest friends, who was among that small group of girls, called to thank me for my spiritual encouragement so many years ago.

The author of Hebrews gave a charge to Christians like you and me to come alongside others to encourage them: "Let us think of ways to motivate one another to acts of love and good works. And let us not neglect our meeting together, as some people do, but encourage one another, especially now that the day of his return is drawing near" (Hebrews 10:24-25, NLT). God's grace enables us to fulfill our God-given purpose to encourage, inspire, motivate, and stir up love and good works with people in our sphere. When I was challenged to live in light of this biblical truth, I passed it on to others like my good friend, who faithfully uses her gifts and opportunities to encourage the people she connects with.

In this passage, the author further explains that encouragement takes place when we get together with other Christians. In our Bible study, we not only experienced encouragement as we met regularly but also discovered that this truth of "meeting together" motivated unchurched college students to recognize the importance of attending a local congregation.

Whether or not people in your life encourage you, the pages of the Bible are full of ample spiritual encouragement. The Psalms draw us to God's heart and encourage our own hearts. In the Gospels, we're impacted by Jesus' life and teachings. We learn what love is in 1 Corinthians 13 and 1 John 3, and we learn how to protect ourselves with spiritual armor in Ephesians 6.

There were seasons in my life when the Bible was my primary source of spiritual encouragement, and it proved to be exactly what I needed. "All Scripture is inspired by God and profitable for teaching, for reproof, for correction, for training in righteousness, so that the man [and woman] of God may be adequate, equipped for every good work" (2 Timothy 3:16-17).

Don't wait for someone to encourage you! You can be the one to initiate the ripple effects of spiritual encouragement. When a passage or a verse takes on special meaning to you, pass on the encouragement to a friend, coworker, or family member. Don't keep life-changing truth to yourself.

Focusing on the impact I can have on others when I offer spiritual encouragement inspires me to share enthusiastically the truths I'm learning—just like I did when I read the Bible for the first time. God can use our words to encourage those around us to read the Bible's inspired words for themselves. Another aspect of the gift of spiritual encouragement is that when we encourage people in our spheres to deepen their walk with God, they will be inspired to encourage people in theirs.

We can't keep the gift of encouragement to ourselves. Wrap it up and give it away at every opportunity God gives you. Spiritual encouragement really is a gift that keeps on giving!

REFLECTION

Meditate on Hebrews 10:24-25, then put it into practice: Get together regularly with other Christians to encourage one another in your faith. Attend a local church. Join a small group. Meet for lunch with your Christian sisters. Start a Bible study or prayer group in your neighborhood or office. Ask the Lord to enable you to provide spiritual encouragement to someone today so they can grow in their relationship with Him.

40

I BELIEVE

IN PREPARATION TO SPEAK TWICE on faith at a women's conference, I reviewed my bulky binder full of notes on the subject. Faith was one my first speaking topics, probably because life's challenges forced me to learn all I could about trusting God. And I'm still learning. It's an ongoing challenge to apply the truths of faith to the realities of life.

I learned the most about faith from my husband. Bob's life illustrates walking by faith and trusting God for His purpose and His plans, and he has influenced more people than I can count to do the same. Bob's faith has impacted our family in ways I cannot express in words. We've watched him live what he believes about the God he serves, and his faith has not wavered since his diagnosis of Parkinson's disease.

After I spoke about faith on the first night of the conference, I woke up much too early Saturday morning and grabbed a pen. I can't explain it, but I sensed the Lord enabling me to write the poem below. Initially my goal was to inspire my audience, but I quickly realized that "I Believe" was for my husband and for all who need encouragement to keep walking by faith, even when life is hard.

I Believe

When life seems more than I can bear
And I question, "Does anyone care?"
When the burden's so great
That I bend from the weight—
I believe.

When waves of doubt envelop me,
Can I trust a God I cannot see?
When I'm tempted to sin,
To give up and give in—
I believe.

When storm clouds hide the sun,
I lose a race I should have won.
When there's heartache and fear
And no one to cheer—
I believe.

When the enemy whispers lies
And the world screams, "Compromise!"
When I'm weary from the fight,
With no relief in sight—
I believe.

When my dreams go unfulfilled,
The cynic's voice cannot be stilled
When they tell me I should dread
The road that lies ahead—
I believe.

When my strength is nearly gone
And I struggle to go on,
When I stumble in pain,
Will I get up again?
I believe.

I believe Jesus died for me;
Faith in Him has set me free;
And I'll never walk alone
On my path that leads me home.
I believe.

I believe my hope's secure
And life's trials I can endure,
Because heaven's a real place
Where sin and pain He'll erase—
I believe.

No matter how long we've been Christians, we all have moments when we struggle to trust God. In Mark 9, we read about a father who came to Jesus with his son, who was afflicted with a spirit that frequently threw him on the ground and made him unable to talk. The disciples had tried to cast out the spirit but failed. When Jesus told the father that all things were possible for those who believe, the father cried out, "I do believe; help my unbelief" (Mark 9:24). Most of us can relate to the father's candor!

The Lord may not right every wrong here on earth, but faith enables us to trust His plans for us. And like the father in the story, when circumstances are overwhelming and our faith wavers, we can be honest about our struggles and cry out to the Lord, "I do believe; help my unbelief."

REFLECTION

What do you do when your faith is shaken? God can handle our questions, frustrations, and doubts, and He wants us to run into His spiritual arms rather than turn away from Him. In His presence, we are free to ask Him to strengthen our faith. Find Bible passages to encourage and inspire you to trust God. My favorites are in the Psalms. This week, choose a different psalm to read and meditate on every day. Underline a special verse or passage, or write one on a note card to help you recall that God is trustworthy!

We may fail,

but God's love never fails.

Only when we comprehend the

depth of His love are we free to

love ourselves and others.

41

EVERY DAY IS
VALENTINE'S DAY!

IT'S A DAY WHEN RED ROSES grace businesses and homes, heart-shaped cards fill backpacks and in-boxes, chocolate calories don't count, and restaurants have waiting lists. As a child, I viewed love through the lens of Valentine's Day, something that's celebrated once a year before life returns to normal.

I was twelve when I heard for the first time that God loved me. First John 4:10 gives us a beautiful picture of God's love: "In this is love, not that we loved God, but that He loved us and sent His Son to be the propitiation for our sins." My decision to accept His great sacrifice of love on my behalf impacted my eternity, but for too many years, I doubted God's love.

Bob and I made teaching our children about the love of God a priority. "God is love" (1 John 4:16) was the first verse they learned, and the second was "[God's] banner over me is love" (Song of Solomon 2:4). The word *banner* in this verse comes from the Hebrew word *dagal*, meaning "to flaunt" or "raise a flag," or, figuratively, "to be conspicuous."[4] Our love-starved world desperately needs to see a flag flaunting God's conspicuous love for every one of us. The fact that our "love flags" often fly at half-mast or remain neatly folded signifies the enemy's attempts to create doubts about our security in God's love.

The focus of this devotion changed when I stopped writing so I could answer a call from a dear elderly woman. Years ago, her son was tricked by the enemy into believing that God no longer loved him, and he ended his own life. Even though he will see his family again in heaven, he will miss weddings, grandchildren, and opportunities to positively influence others' lives. My friend called me because she was grieving and needed encouragement. I tread softly when I deal with this issue, but if you or someone you love struggles with doubting God's love, you may need encouragement too!

None of us deserve God's love, because we are all sinners. I've met with women who had a past that included lies, an affair, jail time, an abortion, substance abuse, and more. Each one needed help, healing, and the assurance that Jesus died for every sin she would ever commit. The enemy tries to deceive us into believing God can't possibly love us because of something we've done. We can all fill in the blank. But God's forgiveness removes our sins as far as the east is from the west (see Psalm 103:12), and He remembers them no more. He forgives, and He forgives again, and He never stops loving us. "If we confess our sins, He is faithful and righteous to forgive us our sins and to cleanse us from all unrighteousness" (1 John 1:9).

If you are dealing with hard things like depression or doubting God's love, please get help from a Christian counselor. The absolute certainty of God's love must replace wrong thinking. I still remember the day I let go of my doubts about God's love. I was halfway through a women's Bible study at church when our assignment included reading Isaiah 54:10: "'The mountains may be removed and the hills may shake, but My lovingkindness will not be removed from you, and My covenant of peace will not be shaken,' says the LORD who has compassion on you." As I read the verse over and over, God's compassion and love overwhelmed me, and at last I was able to relinquish my doubts about His unconditional love. I sensed unmistakable peace that although circumstances may change, God's love for me would never be removed. I was finally free!

We may fail, but God's love never fails (see 1 Corinthians 13:8). Only when we comprehend the depth of His love are we free to love ourselves and others (see 1 John 4:11).

Whether or not we receive expressions of love such as cards, flowers, and candy, our heavenly Father gives the greatest gift of all: His infinite love. Romans 8:38-39 tells us that nothing can ever separate us from His love. Nothing!

> I am convinced that neither death, nor life, nor angels, nor principalities, nor things present, nor things to come, nor powers, nor height, nor depth, nor any other created thing, will be able to separate us from the love of God, which is in Christ Jesus our Lord.

Remind yourself every day that God really loves you, and thank Him for His love. Fly your "love flag" high! Love is everyone's greatest need, and those of us who have been impacted by God's love are commissioned to serve as His ambassadors to share His love. Don't wait for Valentine's Day!

REFLECTION

What about yourself or your past makes you doubt God's love for you? Look up verses about God's love and write them down in a journal or in places where you will see them frequently. Choose one to memorize so the truth of God's love is readily accessible. Review them whenever you begin to question whether God really loves you.

42

THE STRESS OF STRESS

WE LIVE IN A WORLD replete with stress. We carry it with us like we do our purses, and it makes our heads throb, our hearts beat faster, and our stomachs ache. But none of us have room in our already full lives for this demanding, uninvited guest that consumes our thoughts, energy, and time, wreaking havoc without hindrance.

This sense of anxiety is more prevalent now than it was in past generations. The increase is due, in part, to nonstop news coverage of violence, tragedies, natural disasters, political outrage, and much more. With bad news from around the world added to our own responsibilities, we can't seem to avoid the onslaught of stress! We wish there were a pill, a shot, or an alternative course of action to relieve it.

Stress can lead to very real physical issues. In fact, it is one of the leading causes of women's health issues such as headaches, high blood pressure, and heart problems. However, it is also a spiritual issue. Psychologists agree that anxiety levels are impacted by an individual's coping mechanisms, including family, friends, and spiritual resources like the Bible. You probably already know my favorite "coping with stress" passage:

> Do not be anxious about anything, but in every situation, by prayer and petition, with thanksgiving, present your requests to God. And the peace of God, which transcends all understanding, will guard your hearts and your minds in Christ Jesus.
> PHILIPPIANS 4:6-7, NIV

In these two verses, the apostle Paul prescribes a directive to slow the spinning of our busy lives: "Do not be anxious about anything." Everything we deal with that creates stress and anxiety fits in the category of *anything*. And then he adds the critical word *but*, which connects us to our alternative to anxiety: We have the privilege of talking to the Lord in prayer about *everything* stressful (naming the specifics) and asking for His help. He already knows what we need, and those needs draw us to the only One who has the power to meet them.

Then, by faith, Paul encourages us to thank the Lord, because He cares about our *everything*.

As I was in the final stages of editing my first book, *Ripple Effects*, my husband decided to do his part to eliminate my stress and planned a getaway using frequent flyer miles and hotel points. Of course, packing, planning, and checking off the long to-do list before leaving home also creates stress—head-bursting stress for this OCD girl! Just before leaving for the airport, I was printing my manuscript to take with me when my printer suddenly stopped. I cried as we hurried out the door. It wasn't until I settled in my seat on the plane that I remembered the solution to my stress. Why do I do everything else before I pray? I finally quoted my verses and gave the Lord my stress, my manuscript, our trip, and everything else that came to mind. And just like He promised, He gave me His unmistakable peace. My shoulders lowered, and I took a breath.

When we got to our connecting airport, Bob helped me find a business center where I could print the rest of my manuscript. An employee offered to assist me, and while the pages were printing, I asked her about her life. She poured out her heart while I prayed silently. I asked whether she had a relationship with the Lord, and she responded that she didn't know that was possible. When the printer finished its job, she returned to hers.

As only the Lord could arrange, our flight was delayed. An

hour later, the young woman found me. With tears in her eyes, she whispered, "I read this on my break," and she pointed to the small tract I had given her. "You are right—God loves me. He really loves me, and He will help me with my stress like He helps you with yours. He sent you to tell me. I asked Jesus to be my Savior." We hugged, I prayed for her, and we talked about seeing each other again in heaven. And then I cried again, but not from stress. I almost missed this incredible opportunity because stress was making life all about me. Peace makes life all about the Prince of Peace!

Desperation to rid ourselves of the heavy weight of stress draws us closer to our mighty God. The result of giving God everything stressful is a supernatural peace, the opposite of anxiety. What a great trade!

REFLECTION

Write Philippians 4:6-7 on a note card and carry it with you in your purse; then work to memorize the passage so you can carry it with you in your heart, ready to apply it to life's stressful situations. Ask the Lord to take your stresses and to give you His peace instead.

43

A GOOD NAME

Baby-name books were introduced around the time Bob and I became parents. We spent hours discussing possible choices before each child was born. As the kids grew up, we talked to them about why we chose their specific names and the importance of a "good name."

Names are also significant to the Lord. Throughout the Bible, the leading characters often have meaningful names, which were occasionally changed to fit their position and circumstances. For example, the name *Abram* means "exalted father," but God changed Abram's name to *Abraham*—which means "father of many"—to underscore God's promise that Abraham would have more descendants than he could count.

As I mentioned earlier, our family read a chapter from the

book of Proverbs every day for many years. Numerous subjects are addressed in King Solomon's book of wisdom, including names: "A good name is to be more desired than great wealth, favor is better than silver and gold" (Proverbs 22:1). We had many lively discussions around our breakfast table on the importance of earning and keeping a good name.

Our reputations attach to our names like shadows that follow us wherever we go. With our names, we represent our families. And if we are Christians, we also represent Christ as His ambassadors to the world. The responsibility to honor the names of our families and of our God should be taken seriously. Onlookers will form their opinions of both by what they see and hear from us.

When your name is mentioned, what do you imagine pops into the minds of hearers? Are they likely to think of you as kind, arrogant, loyal, hardworking, critical, encouraging, trustworthy, harsh, or joyful? Your influence is connected to your actions, which expose your character and determine whether you have a good or bad name. If you have a good name, Proverbs 22:1 implies that you are blessed to have favor with the people in your sphere. And although the plot of countless books and movies is the pursuit of wealth, this verse makes the case that the pursuit of a good name, and the favor that accompanies it, is a much more worthwhile quest.

When I first began my walk with the Lord in college, one of the few Christians I knew rarely smiled and had a noticeably critical spirit. She was quick to judge my first steps as a young believer. The girls who lived around us based their opinion of Christ on her and ended up with a negative view. Thankfully I had another Christian friend, Michelle, who was enthusiastic about her faith and encouraged my feeble efforts to grow in mine. My goal became to influence others for Christ like she was influencing me.

Representing Jesus is an opportunity for eternal influence that we shouldn't take lightly. People watch us to see whether He is making a difference in our lives. Our decisions, actions, and words impact the name of our Savior.

We cautioned our children about the serious consequences of tarnishing their good names. The news is filled with stories of well-known people who have ruined their names and reputations—celebrities, politicians, business executives, sports heroes, and even religious leaders. It's almost impossible to restore the reputation of one's name once it's damaged. This warning should cause us to focus on protecting our names like we protect our prized possessions. Although it's important to prioritize our jobs, homes, savings, investments, and valuables, Proverbs 22:1 teaches that a more consequential priority is to protect our good names, which give us favor with both God and men.

A children's story we read to our kids about the integrity of George Washington and his "do right" rule[5] provided practical ways to protect our good names: tell the truth, guard our tongues, and treat people like we want to be treated. But we discovered an even higher standard for a good name in 1 Corinthians 10:31: "Whether, then, you eat or drink or whatever you do, do all to the glory of God." *Glory* in this verse implies that our words and actions should make God look good and enhance His name and reputation.

In the last chapter of the Bible, Revelation 22, we are told that at the end of time, we will see the face of our Savior, and His name—the greatest of all names—will be on our foreheads (see verse 4). What a privilege to honor His name now in our circles of influence!

REFLECTION

Take a minute to consider how others might view you. How do you think the way you live reflects on God's good name? Memorize Proverbs 22:1 this week, and review it often to remind yourself of the importance of establishing and maintaining a good name. Ask the Lord to enable you to represent Him well and influence the people you care about to do the same.

THE STORMS OF LIFE

As I write this devotion, the east coast of Florida is preparing for a category 5 hurricane. We know the drill: stock up on bottled water and nonperishable food; make sure the flashlights and generator are working; and fill up the gas tanks in our cars. We take the warnings seriously and prepare.

Are you prepared for a major storm? Your storm might not be nature related, like a hurricane, tornado, fire, flood, or earthquake. It could be physical, spiritual, emotional, relational, or financial. And whether the category of your storm is a one or a ten, it's important to be prepared.

Years ago, I sat in a hospital waiting room in the Philippines while my young daughter Katie had surgery. We were so far from home, and I felt alone. My eyes began to fill with tears. Only God could hear my silent cry, and I begged the Lord to direct me to a passage that would encourage me in the midst of my storm. As I flipped through the pages of my Bible, my compassionate God answered my simple prayer with special verses for that storm and many storms to come.

Psalm 62:5-8 has become my security passage, the place I run to when a storm is approaching. As I sat alone in the waiting room that day, I memorized its life-impacting verses. Although I often put verses to common tunes, this was a special passage, so I asked the Lord for a special tune. I can't explain how it happened, but by the time I was allowed to see my daughter, the verses and the tune were mine.

> My soul, wait in silence for God only,
> For my hope is from Him.
> He only is my rock and my salvation,
> My stronghold; I shall not be shaken.
> On God my salvation and my glory rest;
> The rock of my strength, my refuge is in God.
> Trust in Him at all times, O people;
> Pour out your heart before Him;
> God is a refuge for us.
>
> PSALM 62:5-8

These verses draw me to God alone: my rock, salvation, stronghold, strength, glory, and refuge. I can trust Him with every challenge and pour out my heart to Him anytime, all the time. As thankful as I am for my family, friends, pastors, and resources, God is my source of real hope, the only One who can prevent the circumstances of life from shaking my faith.

Even when our walk with the Lord is stable and our faith is strong, we can still be shaken by a storm. Luke, author of one of the Gospels and the book of Acts, related firsthand how he and 275 other ship passengers lost hope during a storm on the Mediterranean Sea (see Acts 27:20, 37). The incredible aspect of this story is that the apostle Paul was in the ship with them, yet they still lost hope. As helpful and encouraging as the Christians in our lives can be, we cannot place our faith in people; they are human and fallible like we are.

Anyone can lose hope when a storm rages. Our emotions can rise and fall like the waves of the sea that nearly capsized the ship in this story. The crew was forced to jettison cargo and run the vessel aground on the island of Malta. A sea, like our circumstances, can transition from calm to rough in a matter of minutes. That's also true of our health, finances, relationships, plans, and dreams. Our faith must rely on God and His steadfast Word, which is inspired, reliable, and unchangeable! Paul encouraged every passenger and member of the crew to keep up their courage during the storm. Our supernatural courage results from the security that God gives and has promised in His Word. Read it, memorize it, engraft it, count on it!

We need to prepare for our storms now, before we hear the forecast, receive the test results, or open the email. Before more time and more storms pass. The news outlets are helpful, but the forecast changes as often as we change the channel. Our unchanging, sovereign, trustworthy God has worked through men to write a book packed with inspired words that give us hope in the midst of life's storms. We can prepare now by choosing verses we can cling to when hurricane-force winds blow our way.

REFLECTION

I'm not blessed with a great voice, but when a storm is forecast, I can lay my head on my pillow and sing my verses to the Lord, and somehow that's enough! My heart is drawn to the Lord, the source of peace, hope, forgiveness, love, strength, courage, and more. Are you prepared for the approaching storm? Find "your" security verses, and then work to memorize them. Putting them to a tune isn't necessary, but you might enjoy the process.

45

THE CIRCLE OF GENEROSITY

WE DON'T NEED A BIG INCOME to be generous! Material possessions aren't necessary either. Generosity is a mindset we form
when we make conscious choices to share our resources with
those who need assistance, support, or love. In responding to
a need, we make a decision to help. When we make an impact
through a generous act as small as sending a birthday card or as
big as providing for a financial need, we create a ripple effect, a
circle of generosity. One generous act can inspire more acts of
generosity, and the circle widens.

My husband's lifelong example taught our family the joy
of generosity. I don't remember witnessing generosity in action

before I met Bob. My parents gave out of abundance, but I have learned that it's possible to give when you don't have excess—and have fun in the process. Our children watched their dad exhibit both wisdom and generosity with whatever resources God provided at the time. In 1991, he started an orphanage in the Philippines with a small inheritance, and through the years it has served as home to hundreds of children. A few years later, in Florida, he invited young men with varied issues to live rent-free in our modest detached apartment.

Bob's "giving" verse is the first Scripture I ever put to a tune: "Give, and it will be given to you; good measure, pressed down, shaken together, running over, they will pour into your lap. For by your standard of measure it will be measured to you in return" (Luke 6:38).

Each of our children widened the circle with his or her unique opportunities for generous acts. One of my favorite illustrations is from our missionary daughter and son-in-law, who lived in a dark place at the time. Thanksgiving was not, of course, celebrated in the country where they served, but it was a reminder to share God's blessings with others.

Together with some other missionary families, they decided to minister to the many beggars in their city. The men borrowed a van and drove through the streets picking up people who were out begging, many of whom were crippled. While the men bathed the beggars and dressed them in new clothes, the women prepared food for a special meal.

One sweet side story is the concern of these homeless people for their friends. They told the men where to find every beggar in their city so our son-in-law and his friends could find anyone they had missed the first time.

After all the guests were clean and full, they were given a Bible and invited to take part in the Thanksgiving service with the missionary families. Many came to know Jesus. "Beggars Baptist Church" is the nickname for the church that started that day and still exists.

The generosity that inspired this story resulted from gratitude. As the missionary families focused on their many blessings that Thanksgiving morning, they were inspired to share their blessings with the less fortunate. We don't need to wait for Thanksgiving. Thank the Lord now for your blessings! Ask Him to make you alert to needs that you can meet by sharing what God has given you.

Maybe you're already being generous with the resources God has provided. As you continue to share your blessings, you'll have the promise of eternal dividends in return. Paul writes in Philippians 4:19, "My God will supply all your needs according to His riches in glory in Christ Jesus."

Or you may be more like me—naturally cautious and frugal.

We can learn to give as the biblical perspective that God supplies enough for our needs—and enough to share—transforms us from selfish to generous. When we know firsthand the generosity of our God, we can, with real conviction, influence others to join the circle of generosity.

REFLECTION

Can you identify a few needs you think God might be calling you to help meet by sharing what you have? For inspiration, read about the generosity of the Macedonians in 2 Corinthians 8–9, particularly in the following verses:

> You must each decide in your heart how much to give. And don't give reluctantly or in response to pressure. "For God loves a person who gives cheerfully." And God will generously provide all you need. Then you will always have everything you need and plenty left over to share with others. As the Scriptures say, "They share freely and give generously to the poor. Their good deeds will be remembered forever."
>
> 2 CORINTHIANS 9:7-9, NLT

46

THE SUPERPOWER
OF FORGIVENESS

I was stunned when I received the call. *They took what was intended to be mine! How could my extended family be so deceitful?* I wondered. While I was living on the opposite coast, they had concocted an elaborate scheme to change my grandmother's will.

I enjoyed a special relationship with my grandmother through the years. She lived with my sister and me for months when my mother stayed by my father's side in Walter Reed Hospital in Washington, DC. My dad, an army colonel, had a life-threatening heart issue related to his service during the Korean War. Grandma attended my special events and was very involved in my life. She was delighted when I married Bob, and she loved being part of our wedding festivities. Although I never inquired, my grandmother often mentioned that her sizable estate would be divided evenly between her six grandchildren. But when she died, my sister and I were only awarded one hundred dollars apiece. I never received my check and later learned that while my grandmother was dying, she was forced to sign a new will, one she was too ill to even read.

Bob and I had only been married two years, were attending grad school, and had no optional resources or time to fight. We certainly could have used the money. We prayed, sought counsel, called an attorney, and prayed some more. After weighing our options, we decided on a radical choice—we would forgive and let it go. I never saw my offenders again.

Forgiveness was still a new concept for me at the time. When I was growing up, I never knew it was an option. It was not my go-to response in situations involving offenses or injustices. Actually, it wasn't my go-to response at all.

When I first found out about the theft, I did what came naturally—I became angry. Anger turned to bitterness, which consumed my life for a day or two. Unwilling to forgive, I was in bondage for a short time, awarding the thieves a double victory. At first Bob had been angry, too, but then he began to reflect on forgiveness. He learned that in the original Greek of the New Testament, which he was studying at the time, one word used for *forgive* means "releasing someone from obligation or debt."[6] And we didn't need to look hard to find applicable Scripture on forgiveness in our Bibles. This verse from the Lord's Prayer was a good place to begin: "Forgive us our debts, as we also have forgiven our debtors" (Matthew 6:12).

Bob and I prayed together, admitting to the Lord how challenging it was for us to forgive and walk away. I still remember how amazing it felt when we laid the offense and the people involved at the foot of the cross. We experienced the incredible results of forgiving the offenders—freedom, peace, and the ability to move on and not look back.

When we forgive offenses, our enemy, the devil, might try to dredge them up and place the portraits of the offenders back in the galleries of our minds. That happened in our case. But Bob and I recognized the source and agreed together that the offense was buried and no longer controlled us. As my grandson might shout, "Forgiveness is an incredible superpower"—a superpower that erases the memory of an injustice. It works so well that I had forgotten about this incident until I asked the Lord to remind me of a long-ago offense I could use in this devotion.

Is there someone you need to forgive—a parent; your husband or child; a friend, boss, or neighbor? Often people closest to us hurt us the most. How can you and I forgive those who have gossiped about us, crushed our spirits, treated us unfairly, or taken what is rightfully ours?

Reconciliation is a welcome gift, but it's one our offenders may not choose to give. Whether or not our relationships with the offenders are fully repaired or restored, forgiveness is God's great gift to us, made possible by His Son, Jesus. It really is a superpower. In the same way that God forgives our offenses against Him, we must also do the same for others: "Forgiving each other, whoever has a complaint against anyone; just as the Lord forgave you, so also should you" (Colossians 3:13).

REFLECTION

Read the story of the unforgiving debtor in Matthew 18:21-35. What do you take away from this parable that you can apply to your life? Select a few key verses from this passage to meditate on this week, or choose from 130-plus other Bible verses on forgiveness. If you have someone in your life you need to forgive, consider how holding on to their offense has affected you. How do you think you could be changed if you were able to let it go? Pray that God would help you to forgive so you can experience His freedom.

47

RESCUED

"SIR, I HAVE GIRLS TO SELL! VERY CHEAP!" When the sleazy man approached my husband on the street, Bob's only thought was that he must rescue the girls. He quickly reached for his wallet and purchased all of them. The youngest was only five.

This sovereign rescue occurred years ago in a semiclosed country where our family ministers. Since then, many girls have been rescued, not only from a life of trafficking but also from worshiping the evil gods of their country's religion. By the grace of our loving God and the help of our son Tim's foundation, we built a beautiful safe house that serves as a boarding school and a home to many rescued girls. Each year when we visit, the incredible transformation in the girls touches our hearts like few other life experiences. With the support of loving Christian houseparents, the girls become more secure and less fearful. They begin to believe that they are safe, loved by God, and accepted by other believers.

Rescue is a theme for my life too. I was never trafficked, but I needed to be rescued. The Greek word for *to rescue* is also translated *to save* or *to deliver*. I was saved and delivered from a vain, self-absorbed life, focused on the worship of me. If you know Jesus, then you were rescued from the clutches of the enemy too. Colossians 1:13-14 tells us, "He rescued us from the domain of darkness, and transferred us to the kingdom of His beloved Son, in whom we have redemption, the forgiveness of sins." Bob paid a few hundred dollars for each girl, but our God sacrificed the life of His Son to rescue you and me. Our response to the One who rescued us from life apart from Him should be overwhelming gratitude and the determination to cry for continued rescue when we are in trouble.

There are many verses in the Psalms that deal with God rescuing people who cry out to Him. When I need rescuing, I have two favorite verses that I pray. One is Psalm 31:2: "Incline Your ear to me, rescue me quickly; be to me a rock of strength, a stronghold to save me." The other is Psalm 50:15:

"Call upon Me in the day of trouble; I shall rescue you, and you will honor Me."

I take this last verse literally and call on the Lord to rescue me every day, many times a day. This week, for example, the Lord rescued me when I misplaced something important. When I couldn't recall a person's name. When I was exhausted and needed energy to keep going. When I needed grace to ignore a critical comment. When I needed to give edifying messages at two events. When I spent a rare free Saturday catching up on paperwork and needed help to combat my tendency to complain.

I also require daily rescue from pride, vanity, selfishness, impatience, negative attitudes, and thoughtless speech. In response to His rescue, I'm very aware of God's involvement in every aspect of my life. My heartfelt response is to give Him the glory He alone deserves.

Each time Bob and I visit the safe house for rescued girls, we bring the girls a variety of gifts, both necessities and special treats. In preparation for our visit, they prepare songs in English to express their gratitude. I leave convicted that I don't always thank the Lord for rescuing me. When I focus on the grace He freely gives to someone like me who did nothing to deserve it, I have a desire to pass His grace on to others—just like we pass out gifts to our precious rescued girls.

REFLECTION

Memorize Psalm 31:2, Psalm 50:15, or another favorite "rescue verse" to take with you wherever you go in life as a reminder that God is always ready to help you. What have you already been rescued from? Take time to thank the Lord for rescuing you from your past and also for His plans "to give you a future and a hope" (Jeremiah 29:11). Then remind yourself that He is standing by to rescue you every moment of every day. Apply this great truth to your life today and share God's rescue plan with the people you love.

48

GOD IS GREAT. GOD IS GOOD. LET US THANK HIM . . .

LAST NIGHT, OUR YOUNGEST SON married his beautiful bride in a God-honoring ceremony, followed by a magical celebration with family and friends. My husband and I had prayed diligently for our son's future wife, and God brought the two together in an obvious display of His grace. He alone deserves all the credit and glory.

But in the midst of the festivities, it would have been easy to overlook who orchestrated the divine match; who made the sun to shine for the outdoor wedding, when there had been heavy rain and strong winds as we went to bed the night before; and who impacted the many guests with compelling evidence of His sovereign presence and preeminence.

When we share specifics

about answered prayers,

people are inspired to believe

that God is willing to answer

their prayers too.

Perhaps you have had a similar experience. God surprised you in a moment of divine intervention, gifted you with the deepest desire of your heart, or enabled you to do what you thought was impossible. Because the Lord answered your prayer, you burst into happy tears, laughed out loud, or shared with anyone who would listen. When things like this happen to us, we often share our amazement and gratitude with others in our excitement, but we might forget to tell the One who answered our prayers just how thankful we are.

Although my illustration is a wedding, a prayer for God's involvement could range from making a plea to find a lost item to begging God to heal a loved one. I have had answers to both and to many prayers in between; yet I am often guilty, I am ashamed to admit, of neglecting to credit the One who answered. But not today!

Prayers for this couple were numerous and the answers extraordinary. It's improbable that two people from different continents would ever connect; and the chances of both being in the same place at the same time, when their responsibilities include constant travel, are even lower. But we should never underestimate the power of the prayers of two families who had prayed for their children's mates since they were born. God used a unique commonality to bring them together: The bride had a sister with special needs who went to be with Jesus a year ago, and the groom has had a heart for people with special needs since he was fifteen, resulting in a worldwide ministry. Everyone close to the couple marvels that God brought together two people with such genuine love and compassion for the special people He created.

There are some occasions when words alone don't seem adequate to express gratitude, and this was one of those times. But I knew immediately where to turn for assistance in expressing thanks. Years before, when God overwhelmed me with His obvious blessing on our oldest daughter's wedding, I discovered a verse I would later use to respond to God's gracious participation and answers to months of prayer. As I walked hand in hand with my husband from our daughter's wedding venue, I quoted this verse over and over: "I will praise you forever, because You have done it; and in the presence of Your saints I will wait on Your name, for it is good" (Psalm 52:9, NKJV). I love this verse! It encourages me to thank the Lord for His efforts on my behalf.

Answered prayers build our faith and reassure us that God loves us. And they also enable us to influence others. When we share specifics about answered prayers, people are inspired to believe that God is willing to answer their prayers too. At a recent women's event, I told a favorite "answer to prayer" story about God providing a dress for my daughter's wedding. It's one I've shared many times, including in my first book,

Ripple Effects. Afterward, I was amazed that nearly every woman in line shared that she couldn't wait to have her own prayer story like my "blue dress" story.

Take a moment to review past answers to your prayers, both small and large. Thank God for them now. If prayer is new to you, begin today to talk to the Lord about your life issues. He already knows what they are, and He cares about every detail. One of my favorite aspects of prayer is that thanking my heavenly Father for who He is and what He has done draws me straight to His throne, where I am transformed by His grace. Hebrews 4:16 reminds us that God is always ready to listen and help: "Let us draw near with confidence to the throne of grace, so that we may receive mercy and find grace to help in time of need."

REFLECTION

Memorize Psalm 52:9 in your favorite translation, or select your own "gratitude" verse. As you know, I often put a special verse to a simple tune to make remembering it easier. Quote or sing your verse to the Lord when He answers your prayer, and then share enthusiastically about God's love and faithfulness with people in your life.

49

GOOD NEWS OF GREAT JOY

THE DAY AFTER CHRISTMAS, my husband and I boarded a plane to fly home after a family gathering. When we discovered our seats were split up, even though our itinerary indicated otherwise, we knew what that meant: God had someone He wanted one of us to talk to. We weren't able to sit together on the flight to our destination, either, and Bob had shared his faith with the young Buddhist woman he sat next to. Now it was my turn.

Oh, Lord, I prayed, *I am tired, but here she is.*

"How are you?" I asked my stylish seatmate. After several minutes of casual conversation, she closed her book and shared her story. As I listened to her struggles and contemplated my response, the verses that had gripped my heart during that Christmas season flashed in my mind:

> The angel said to them, "Do not be afraid; for behold, I bring you *good news of great joy* which will be for all the people; for today in the city of David there has been born for you a Savior, who is Christ the Lord."
>
> LUKE 2:10-11, EMPHASIS ADDED

We talked awhile, and I shared that we can still have joy even when things don't go our way—joy that comes from knowing Christ. The instant our dialogue flipped to spiritual things, my seatmate lost interest and returned to her book. When she comes to mind now, I pray that someday she will find real joy in a relationship with Jesus.

Do you have great joy? I asked myself the same question when I woke up this morning and looked in the mirror. My countenance revealed no sign of joy, great or small. The much-anticipated plans for my day had been cancelled, so I needed a transfusion of joy before I said good morning to anyone.

Where should we turn when life doesn't go our way? We know the answer; yet sometimes I pout rather than open my Bible. Today, though I was disappointed, I turned to where I left off yesterday, in the book of Jeremiah. The Old Testament prophet continually dealt with difficult and unfair circumstances. I am both intrigued and convicted that when Jeremiah ached because of his persecutors and was distraught about what was happening to his people, he wrote, "Your words were found and I ate them, and Your words became for me a joy and the delight of my heart; for I have been called by Your name, O Lord God of hosts" (Jeremiah 15:16).

In this passage, Jeremiah compares God's Word to food. We rarely ignore our need for physical food, but it's our human nature to disregard the spiritual food found in our God-given manual for life. Yet supernatural words on the pages of the inspired Word of God can draw us straight to the heart of God, our source of joy. It happened to me today as my hunger for encouragement was satisfied while I feasted on truth.

Our enemy comes to steal, kill, and destroy our joy, but our defense is the Word of God. This side of heaven, we need to resist our tendency to nibble on lesser things and instead fill our minds and hearts with the substantive spiritual food found in the pages of the Bible. Just as regular meals are an essential part of our routines, making time to read the Bible should also be routine. The enemy doesn't care if we eat, but he will do everything in his power to keep us from being impacted by the powerful Word of God and finding joy through its truth. May the joy of the Lord be our strength!

REFLECTION

Prepare yourself to impact others with your joy by beginning each day with time in God's Word. When the Bible was new to me, I started reading in Philippians, a book full of references to joy. While Paul was under arrest for preaching the gospel and was awaiting trial in a Roman prison, he demonstrated what real joy looks like. He shared his joy with the Philippians and encouraged them to share their joy with him (see Philippians 2:17-18).

Even when we know our source of joy, at times we still sense that joy slipping away. The good news is that God, through His Spirit and His Word, will fill us with great joy again and again, and one day, if we know Jesus, we will stand before Him: "Now to Him who is able to keep you from stumbling, and to make you stand in the presence of His glory blameless with great joy, to the only God our Savior, through Jesus Christ our Lord, be glory, majesty, dominion and authority, before all time and now and forever. Amen" (Jude 1:24-25).

50

FINISHING STRONG

It seems there is always a party at my daughter Katie's house, and the weekend of my visit was no exception. We were preparing for a unicorn-themed swim party, and everyone had an assignment. My responsibility was to make colored cake pops to give as favors to the little girls celebrating our sweet Brynn's seventh birthday.

Cake pops were new to me, but I had help from nine-year-old Riley, an experienced cake pop baker. Brynn also assisted and sampled, until her attention span paid no more attention. Riley and I discussed her varied interests as we mixed batter; poured it into the cake pop pan; baked the cake pops; added sticks, icing, and glitter; wrapped each one in plastic; and finally placed the finished pops into designated holes in the cake pop holder. Whew!

What seemed like a fun project at first, complete with yummy dough to lick off our fingers, became a chore as young guests began to arrive. But we still had lots of cake pops to go!

"Riley, as important as it is to start a project, it's equally important to finish it," I encouraged her. "You and Grandma need to be 'finishers.'"

"What's a 'finisher,' Grandma?" she asked.

"A finisher doesn't quit an assignment because it's demanding," I responded. "Anyone can begin, but only finishers can end."

"Wow," she said, smiling as she worked faster. "I guess Brynn isn't a finisher, is she?"

"Let's give Brynn grace today, because it's her birthday," I responded. "You and Brynn are such buddies, and you can help her learn to finish another time. You know who's a good finisher?" I asked her. "Grandpa. He has more challenges now with Parkinson's, but he still travels to faraway places, where he tells people about Jesus. His legs really hurt, but he doesn't complain because he is determined to be a finisher!"

When the last of the pops were ready to bake, I sent Riley to greet more guests and thanked her for her help. Then big sister Abby saved the day by covering our droopy cake pops with decorations.

As I prepared to fly home the next day, Riley and I hugged. "Grandma, I'm a finisher like Grandpa, aren't I?" she said with a smile.

"You certainly are, Riley. I'm so proud of you! Grandpa will be proud, too, when I tell him you didn't quit on your responsibility."

Are you a finisher? Most of our assignments are harder than making cake pops, and it's natural to get discouraged and give up before we're done. We're tempted to quit on marriage when we clash with our mates. We might quit school when the coursework becomes too challenging or quit jobs when we don't get raises or recognition. We quit putting our best effort into parenting because the task is too demanding. We sometimes quit church over minor issues or quit loving people who offend us. We quit because of selfishness, laziness, bitterness, or pride. All of us struggle to keep going and finish strong.

When Jesus knew His assignment on earth was accomplished, His last words before He gave up His life on the cross were, "It is *finished*!" (John 19:30, emphasis added). Believers are encouraged to follow His example: "Let us run with endurance the race that is set before us, looking unto Jesus, the author and *finisher* of our faith, who for the joy that was set before Him endured the cross, despising the shame, and has sat down at the right hand of the throne of God" (Hebrews 12:1-2, NKJV, emphasis added).

Paul endured much for the sake of the gospel, and as he neared death, he wrote to his disciple Timothy, "I have fought the good fight, I have *finished* the race, I have kept the faith" (2 Timothy 4:7, NKJV, emphasis added). Few of us will be asked to endure a cross or die a martyr's death, but we represent Jesus well when we work to complete our assignments in this world. Do you have a task to finish? A relationship to mend? A debt to pay? A sin to confess? A promise to keep?

Jesus never left a task undone. He is waiting until He hears from His Father that it is time to finish history. Until that moment, let's determine that we will depend on God's grace to represent His Son, our Savior, and finish strong.

REFLECTION

In what areas are you discouraged and tempted to give up? Pray that God will give you the endurance to finish well—to complete with grace the tasks He has given you. Meditate on one of the above Scriptures in John, Hebrews, or 2 Timothy as you consider the examples of Jesus and Paul, who persevered to the end.

51

ETERNAL SECURITY

WHY AM I UNDERWATER? I wondered. Disoriented, I instinctively waved my arms until I felt the side of the pool. While simultaneously spitting out water and gasping for air, I started to cry for help, which was futile since I was home alone. But I wasn't really alone. I whispered, "Help, Lord!" Suddenly the steps were in reach, and I grabbed the handrail for support. I vaguely remember stumbling through the side door to my bedroom, falling into bed, and pulling the covers over my wet bathing suit.

While processing what had just happened, I cried tears of

There is no greater privilege

and call to action than to share

our hope of eternal security with

everyone who will listen.

gratefulness that the Lord had spared me. But I also thanked Him, because I knew beyond a shadow of a doubt that if I had drowned, I would have gone to heaven. At the time, I didn't realize this was another incident where I had blacked out due to my heart stopping for a brief moment. When doctors later figured out what was happening and I learned of my miracle, I sang verses I'd put to a tune years before. Now they took on new meaning:

Whom have I in heaven but You?
And besides You, I desire nothing on earth.
My flesh and my heart may fail,
But God is the strength of my heart and my portion
forever.
PSALM 73:25-26

A few verses later, the psalmist writes that he can't wait to broadcast the amazing things God has done for him (verse 28). I feel the same way, which is why I share this story.

My family, friends, and doctor forbade me to swim laps again until a pacemaker, regulating the electrical function of my heart, solved my health issue—at least for now. The reality is that death is inevitable for all of us, which makes eternal security our greatest need. We have an enemy who will stop at nothing to steal our hope of heaven. Don't listen to him!

When my mother was close to death, she requested that caregivers read her stories about heaven. The Bible and Randy Alcorn's comprehensive book entitled *Heaven* were her only consolation. Her hope was secure that she would soon make the journey from earth to heaven and have no more pain when she met her Savior face-to-face. But in her early years, she rarely thought about eternal security.

When life is full, it's natural to focus on the here and now rather than on what's to come. It's also a challenge to believe in God and heaven while living in a secular culture. There was a time when I doubted my security in Christ. College textbooks and liberal professors disputed my beliefs with half-truths, which I was unable to refute because of weak theology. By God's grace, however, both Mom and I began to grasp our eternal security when we filled our minds with the transforming truth of God's Word.

I'm writing this devotion in the midst of a worldwide pandemic. My heart aches for everyone impacted by the virus, including my missionary daughter's family. Although they don't doubt their eternal security, they serve people who are without the hope of heaven, people who desperately need to hear the Good News: If we trust Jesus to forgive our sins, we have eternal life, and one day Jesus will return to take us to heaven.

By the time you read this, Lord willing, the pandemic will have passed; yet the importance of the gospel will always remain. We don't need to travel across the world to share our faith. What about your friend, neighbor, relative, or coworker—have they heard the simple gospel message? Are they certain that their final destination is heaven? Are you? Don't base facts on feelings, which fluctuate. "For God so loved the world, that He gave His only begotten Son, that whoever believes in Him shall not perish, but have eternal life." (John 3:16). This is our sure hope!

There is no greater privilege and call to action than to share our hope of eternal security with everyone who will listen:

The testimony is this, that God has given us eternal life, and this life is in His Son. He who has the Son has the life; he who does not have the Son of God does not have the life. These things I have written to you who believe in the name of the Son of God, so that you may know that you have eternal life.

I JOHN 5:11-13

REFLECTION

If you doubt your salvation, spend time reading God's Word to remind yourself of what is true. Then ask God to bring people to mind who need to know His good news. You may have already memorized the three verses above from 1 John, but if not, write them on a card or commit them to memory. Pray for the courage and opportunity to share the gospel with people in your sphere so that they may also experience the joy and assurance of eternal security.

52

HOPE FOR OUR HEARTS

HOPE WAS MY TOPIC for two women's holiday events, a week apart on opposite coasts. Following each one, I greeted women from all walks of life. As I listened to their stories, one woman after another relayed circumstances that had led to her broken heart. In response, I wrote this poem:

My heart is broken,
But you can't see a trace
Of the anguish I feel
Since a smile lights my face.

My heart is broken;
It's crushed, and I know

The pain that I hide
Will eventually show.

My heart is broken;
Yours might be too.
Oh, listen, sweet sister;
I'll share my promise with you.

Our hearts are broken,
But I read in God's Word
That we can have hope;
Our prayers have been heard.

"The LORD is near to the brokenhearted
And saves those who are crushed in spirit."
PSALM 34:18

The women's tales of heartbreak stunned me, yet I encouraged every storyteller with the truth that God not only cares but is also on the scene instantly, offering supernatural hope. I could relate to the women's pain from personal experience, and I could reassure them because God had been faithful to draw me close when my spirit was crushed.

God may not be physically close when our hearts break, but

His presence is real. There is no mistaking God's nearness; no human comfort compares, and He offers us real hope. Most of us identify with the women in this story because we, too, can become disillusioned when our hope is dependent on fluctuating circumstances, feelings, and relationships. Biblical hope, by contrast, is based on the sure promises in God's Word (see Romans 15:4). Over time, as we apply truth about God to the circumstances in our lives, we have hope for our hearts, a hope that does not disappoint (see Romans 5:5).

God offers hope full of promise and substance to brokenhearted women whose spirits are crushed. He saves us from despair and hopelessness and wraps His spiritual arms around us, like a mother wraps her arms around her child who skinned a knee or was bullied at school. The spirits of wounded people are encouraged by the compassion and presence of our God, who loves us and draws near to us. We can cry out with the psalmist, "My flesh and my heart may fail, but God is the strength of my heart and my portion forever" (Psalm 73:26).

Why are we so susceptible to broken hearts? Our hearts are tender, made in the image of God, equipping us to love, serve, and give. But like fine china, soft hearts are easily broken. Only God knows how many of us travel through each day lugging the weight of a broken heart. Even when it seems that no one understands our heartaches, there is Someone who is "greater than our heart and knows all things" (1 John 3:20). Our Savior comprehends the cause of every broken heart, whether it is rejection, loneliness, injustice, disapproval, fear, illness, conflict, disappointment, or some other difficulty.

Jesus had compassion for the pain of the hopeless, rejected woman at the well (see John 4). She was living with her sixth "husband" when she met Jesus. He knew her past, but unlike all the people in her world who kept their distance, Jesus came close and offered her His living water—eternal life. When she drank, she had hope for her thirst, her broken heart, and her future. An encounter with Jesus changes everything! We can say with the psalmist, "My hope is from Him" (Psalm 62:5).

None of us are immune from the pain of a broken heart. Don't wait any longer to bring your heartaches to the Lord and receive His hope. Proverbs 13:12 reminds us that "hope deferred makes the heart sick." God alone enables us to keep from losing heart, and He offers us supernatural healing as we trade our broken hearts for His genuine, powerful, life-changing hope. When people and circumstances cause our tender hearts to break, we can, by faith, place our trust in the person and promises of God (see Psalm 78:7). And as we look ahead to our sure hope of heaven (see 1 Peter 1:13), we trust that in God's hands, the hard things we are facing now are opportunities for growth and grace. Our biblical hope is the dynamic confidence that God will come through. He doesn't just give us hope. As 1 Timothy 1:1 assures us, He *is* our hope!

REFLECTION

Take time now to talk to your Savior about your heart issues. Memorize Psalm 34:18—the verse at the end of the poem—as a reminder that God is with you in your suffering. Then read the story about the woman at the well (John 4:7-30) and tell others, like the woman at the well did, about our God who offers His hope for our heartaches.

ACKNOWLEDGMENTS

THANK YOU to the wonderful women at the Fedd Agency, especially Esther and Whitney, for being my cheerleaders who believe in my passion to encourage women with hope for our hearts.

Thank you to everyone at Tyndale, especially Sarah and Karin, whose consistent support serves as motivation to weave my stories together with beloved Scripture to create devotions, which I pray will encourage and inspire the women who read them.

Thank you to my wonderful family (Bob, Christy, Joey, Katie, Robby, Peter, Casey, Timmy, Demi, and all nine grandchildren) and special friends. You inspire me, star in my stories, and are so dear to my heart!

NOTES

1. Horatio Spafford, "It Is Well with My Soul," 1873, verse 1.
2. John Newton, "Amazing Grace," 1779, verse 1.
3. Thomas Chisholm, "Great Is Thy Faithfulness," 1923, refrain.
4. James Strong, *Strong's Exhaustive Concordance*, s.v. "dagal," accessed July 31, 2020, https://biblehub.com/hebrew/1713.htm.
5. See Laurel Hicks, *Hidden Treasure* (Pensacola, FL: Abeka Books, 1974), 90.
6. HELPS Word-studies, copyright © 1987, 2011 by Helps Ministries, Inc., s.v. "Cognate 859 áphesis," accessed July 31, 2020, https://biblehub.com/greek/859.htm.

ABOUT THE AUTHOR

PAM TEBOW travels and speaks across the country, encouraging audiences to use the incredible influence God has given them to eternally impact their worlds. She is the author of *Ripple Effects: Discover the Miraculous Motivating Power of a Woman's Influence.* Pam has appeared on *Good Morning America, Fox and Friends,* and other shows and podcasts. She has won national awards for her ministry work, including Eagle Forum's Woman of the Year and Witness in the Public Square in 2012, Commission for Women's Inspiring Woman of the Year in 2013, Extraordinary Woman of the Year in 2014, and the National Pro-Life Recognition Award in 2017. Pam graduated with honors from the College of Journalism and Communications at the University of Florida. She and her husband, Bob, live in Florida and have five children and nine grandchildren.

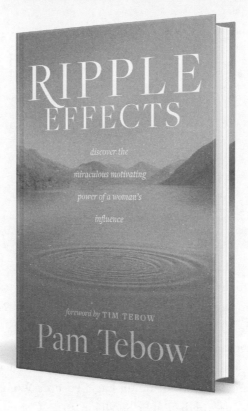

In *Ripple Effects*, Pam Tebow uncovers and explores the miraculous motivating power of influence that we can have on this generation and the next, no matter where we are planted in life. Join Pam as she encourages us to maximize our God-given opportunities for influence—and watch how far the ripples will spread.